REMEMBERING

WADSWORTH

REMEMBERING

WADSWORTH

From PIONEERS *to* STREETCARS

CAESAR A. CARRINO

THE History PRESS

Published by The History Press
Charleston, SC 29403
www.historypress.net

All photographs are courtesy of the Wadsworth Area Historical Society unless otherwise noted.

First published 2009
Second printing 2009

Manufactured in the United States

ISBN 978.1.59629.632.9

Library of Congress Cataloging-in-Publication Data

Carrino, Caesar A., 1931-
Remembering Wadsworth, Ohio : from pioneers to streetcars / Caesar A. Carrino.
p. cm.
Includes bibliographical references.
ISBN 978-1-59629-632-9
1. Wadsworth (Ohio)--History. 2. Wadsworth (Ohio)--Social life and customs. I. Title.
F499.W13C37 2009
977.1'35--dc22
2008055285

Contents

CONTENTS

Contents

FOREWORD

Remembering Wadsworth, Ohio is a compendium of events that took place throughout Wadsworth's nearly two-hundred-year history. Many more episodes are available for presentation, but space constraints made it necessary for the author to limit his offerings. He therefore chose to chronicle only events that were critical to the development of Wadsworth or that were interesting and unique to its history.

In addition to presenting written historical accounts, the author included some facts from interviews conducted for *Wadsworth History on Film*, a program hosted by the author that aired on Wadsworth Public Access Channel WCTV. More than three hundred Wadsworth residents were interviewed, including some descendants of the first families who arrived in 1814. *Wadsworth History on Film* is presented by the Wadsworth Area Historical Society and designed to preserve the oral history of Wadsworth for posterity.

The pioneers, who left the security of a stable life in the East to settle in an untamed virgin forest that rejected them, came with a resolve to dream their visions into reality. They must have felt desperate when they camped on the cold ground on those March nights in 1814, then worked from dawn to dusk, cutting down trees to make logs for their primitive cabins.

How incredible is the resilience of man when hope propels the body beyond its limits. Early settlers languished; they wept, they longed and they suffered. But they did not yield. Instead, they endured. They built, grew, prospered and achieved. And, through their achievements, they made Wadsworth the city that it is today—a monument to the vision of those first settlers.

Here starts this book. Others will write about how Wadsworth will evolve and change, but nothing will change how it was born and evolved. That is history.

Lynda C. Carrino

ACKNOWLEDGEMENTS

The author wishes to acknowledge his wife, Lynda, for her support in promoting the history of Wadsworth, for her role in contributing research for this book and for her active participation in the Wadsworth Area Historical Society. Her career as a historian served as the author's inspiration to become involved in recording local history.

Appreciation is offered also to our son, Michael Carrino, for his computer technology assistance, without which this book would have been written in Spenserian cursive.

Finally, credit is given to the Wadsworth Area Historical Society for supplying the pictures used for the various chronicles.

Part I

Wadsworth Is Born

The First Settlers: Bewildered in the Wilderness

Daniel Dean and Oliver Durham were the first settlers to arrive in the Connecticut Western Reserve, Tract 1, the eastern edge of what is now Wadsworth, named for landowner General Elijah Wadsworth. The Deans and the Durhams were from Vermont and made the trip from there to what is now Western Star by horse and wagon over a span of several weeks.

Wadsworth Memorial (Brown, 1875) states that Daniel and his sons, as well as the Durhams, arrived on March 1, 1814, and set up camp by building a temporary shelter, crafted from big crotched branches and covered with blankets, to protect them from the penetrating March winds.

During their first night, they were greeted by the howls of wolves traveling in packs. Wary, they tried to keep a fire ablaze to stave off the wolves and made periodic noises to scare them away. Succeeding nights brought the same chorus of howls, but now they were becoming accustomed to hearing them and became less concerned about an attack. To this day, the stream that flows on the eastern side of Wadsworth Township and into Norton Township is named Wolf Creek—so named by the Deans and the Durhams when they determined that the wolves followed the creek from its mouth southeast to Chippewa Creek.

During the day, the Deans and the Durhams felled trees, made logs and planks cut by hand, built two cabins—one eighteen by eighteen feet and one eighteen by sixteen feet—and moved into them on March 17, three weeks after arriving. Helping them were Basley Cahow, Jacob Vanhynig (who had only one arm), Indian Holmes (the first "white" settler who married into the Indian community), Theodore Parmelee, George Hethman, James Cahow and George Cahow. The seven helpers came from other settlements to

John Dean, one of the first settlers in Wadsworth, March 1, 1814.

help after hearing that there were newcomers in the adjoining lands. There were only eight houses from Wadsworth to East Akron, a distance of about fifteen miles. All the named helpers lived in one of the eight houses with their families.

Mrs. Dean and Mrs. Durham were the only two women in the new settlement. Of significance is that Mrs. Durham was pregnant during the trip from Vermont to Wadsworth and gave birth to the first child born in Wadsworth, named Alonzo, in July 1814. It was not until months later that another family arrived to join the new settlers, giving the two women other women for company.

A big draw for people to make the treacherous six-hundred-mile trip from Vermont and Connecticut was the price of land: two to five dollars per acre, with deferred payments if the buyer could not afford the total price of the land. Elijah Wadsworth purchased 16,417 acres, slightly more than the usual 16,000 acres allotted to a Connecticut Western Reserve "village" that was five miles square.

The Dean family has had a continuous Wadsworth presence from the days of the first settlers to the present day. Ramona (Edis) Wonov is the oldest survivor of the Dean lineage still living in Wadsworth.

Pioneer Embalmers: The Party's Over

Wadsworth's political climate in the years following the arrival of the first settlers was anything but alive and well. Partisanship was beginning to rise above the tranquility that is usually present when people are striving only to survive. At that level, little concern is afforded ideologies. When basic needs are met, ideologies begin to emerge.

Not too long after the first people brought their families and meager belongings to what would become Wadsworth, settlers began to die. Although most of the early people were self-sufficient and able to build cabins, fell trees, till the soil, preach, govern themselves, teach children, shoe horses, cure the sick, cook, preserve food, make furniture, hunt, define the law, quarry rock and anything else needed for human survival, none knew the art of embalming with any degree of proficiency.

Embalmers were in high demand. All that was needed for a funeral was a casket—always made of wood—a wagon to carry the deceased, a team of horses and an embalmer. This job description would fit almost any adult male with the exception of the last requirement.

A funeral procession coming from north of the square; therefore, the deceased was a Republican.

Ephriam Kremer, great-grandfather of well-known Wadsworth resident Marguerite Kremer Stration (now deceased), and Jonas Wuchter (whose descendants still inhabit Wadsworth) learned how to embalm and became the only two men in the village to achieve this distinction. Both men were of the Pennsylvania Dutch line who inhabited Wadsworth in its formative days and both preserved the hardworking, honest, clannish and somewhat suspicious qualities indigenous to the rest of the Pennsylvania Dutch.

While their values did not wane as they mixed with their sophisticated yet frugal and conservative Connecticut counterparts, some withdrew from the stringent conservatism of their upbringing and swayed toward the Democratic tenets of politics. The Pennsylvania Dutch were straightforward, no-nonsense, honest and hardworking people, but they were somewhat unforgiving when there were schisms in the ranks, especially in political ranks.

Jonas Wuchter, a man known for his strong convictions, elected to remain pure of spirit when dealing with politics. He made beautiful cabinets for the dead, charged little for his services, gave respectful acknowledgements to the bereaved and carried the deceased to the cemetery on time. But he felt that it was important, in order to remain true to his political stand, to embalm only Republicans. This left a fairly sizeable, albeit smaller, segment of the community without embalming services, simply because they were Democrats.

Ephriam Kremer stepped forward. A Pennsylvania Dutchman who swayed a bit from the mainstream of Republican conservatism, Kremer learned to embalm, make beautiful cabinets, acknowledge the bereaved with respect and carry the deceased to the cemetery on time. He was a Democrat, or at least one would suspect, since he deigned to embalm only Democrats.

Thus, with the population being reported only in three figures and the low threes at that, Wadsworth had two embalmers, one at the north end of the Center and one at the south—one for Republicans and one for Democrats.

Both dead.

Sylvia Beach: Lost, Never Found

In 1823, nine years after the Dean and Durham families came to Wadsworth as its first settlers, Abel and Roxy Taylor Beach arrived from the East with their three sons and twenty-three-year-old daughter, Sylvia, to start their new life. Despite the snow and cold temperatures, they began building a cabin by making a small clearing in the woods, shaping the trees into logs for their new shelter.

Sylvia suffered from the effects of scarlet fever as a small child and was a deaf-mute. The disease also affected her mental acuity, causing her to become confused at times. It was not unusual for her to wander from the house, but each time she did, she was either found and returned or returned on her own.

On a fateful day in March 1823, after the cabin was nearly completed and the brush was all but burned to embers, Sylvia slipped away while her mother's back was turned. Both her mother and father called for her, listening for even a faint reply, but there was none. The trees were huge and the underbrush thick, and despite a light coat of snow on the ground, only faint impressions of foot tracks were evident. They followed the tracks but found them to become almost nonexistent as they searched farther from the cabin. Finally, even the hope of a track was not in evidence, either on the ground or in the imaginations of Sylvia's parents.

The location of the cabin was on the north side of what is now Route 261, almost at the top of the hill going west into Wadsworth, where the John Haynes farm still stands. From that point, neighbors searched every direction,

Sylvia Beach's house, from which she disappeared.

but especially to the southwest, where some tracks were spotted, presumably Sylvia's. As night fell, the searchers lighted torches that illuminated the dense woods and continued their search. Being unsuccessful, they enlisted the assistance of other villagers, who came in large numbers to help.

Of particular significance was the fact that the story of the disappearance was of such magnitude that people such as William Eyles—a community leader, associate judge, county commissioner and state representative—presented himself as the commander of the search and called together other notables of the day, including Frederick Brown, Allen Pardee and Sherman Loomis. The newly formed search party trekked every inch of the woods in Wadsworth, Norton, Sharon Center and Copley. Not satisfied with their failure to find her, Eyles ordered the volunteers to search the woods again, even if only to find her body. A week went by, and in consultation with Sylvia's parents and brothers—Abel, George and Orlando—Eyles decided to direct the search back to the cabin and to move every log, stone or leaf in its vicinity before declaring that she was never to be found. They even enlisted the aid of the *Ohio Repository* (Canton) and the *Cleveland Herald*, but to no avail.

Wadsworth commemorated Sylvia's loss for years, but the community's coming together as it did to evince their compassion was the start of a tradition that speaks to what makes Wadsworth a family.

In 1824, the family erected a stone to mark the empty grave with the heart-wrenching words: "Sylvia Beach, Lost in the Woods, and Never Found."

John Brown's Origins: Why He Went by His Middle Name

The Frederick and Chloe Pettione Brown family came to Wadsworth in 1816 and was the first family *inside* the present village corporation. The family was vast and influential, bringing with them notables such as sons Dr. John Brown (not John of Harper's Ferry fame, but a cousin), Dr. Marcus Brown, Reverend Edward Brown and Catharine Brown, who married Timothy Hudson, son of Deacon David Hudson, who founded Hudson, Ohio.

Frederick Brown's brother, Owen Brown, was the father of John Brown, the abolitionist, and the Reverend Edward Brown, who wrote the history of Wadsworth in 1875. Frederick and Owen were both born in Canton, Connecticut, in 1769 and 1771 respectively, and were sons of Captain John Brown and fifth-generation descendants of Peter Brown, who came on the *Mayflower*.

Captain John Brown died in the Revolutionary War in 1776, leaving Chloe and eleven children. Times were hard for the widowed Chloe, and she was forced to have her sons, Frederick and Owen, become the breadwinners. Owen learned the tanner and cobbler trades and passed his skills on to his son, Osawatomie John Brown, the abolitionist movement notable (Osawatomie was one of John's nicknames, but he chose always to go by just John). Owen also had an adopted son, Levi Blakeslee, who opened the first tannery in Wadsworth. Of note, also, is that Owen taught the trades to Jesse Grant, the father of President Ulysses S. Grant.

In 1805, Owen Brown went to live in Hudson, Ohio, but owned land in Wadsworth. While in Hudson, he became the first county commissioner of Portage County, then the county that included what is now Medina County. As commissioner, he exerted much influence and was responsible for building the east–west road through Wadsworth, now Broad and College Streets. This act alone provided facilities for people to settle among the smattering of homes and, in fact, the impetus for growth of the village.

Lasting evidence of Owen Brown's contributions to Wadsworth is the "old ground" of Woodlawn Cemetery, the area on the north side of College Street and the entrance to the rest of the now sprawling cemetery. Owen Brown originally reserved this "ground" as a burial plot for himself and his family members eleven years before he donated it to the Wadsworth Township Trustees for use as a public cemetery. His only requests were that the public pay for a fence and that he and his descendants be able to graze their sheep or other small animals there so long as they did not destroy the integrity of the burial plots. The reason for establishing the family cemetery

Owen Brown, father of John Brown, the abolitionist.

was that Owen's brother, Frederick, lost his infant daughter in 1817—the first to be buried in the "old ground."

Although Owen Brown and his son, Osawatomie John, were Wadsworth visitors on a regular basis, neither lived in Wadsworth. Frederick did live in Wadsworth and became one of its most prominent citizens. Since Frederick was educated and had educated sons, it is thought that he was the dominant brother and uncle to whom others looked for advice and counsel.

In 1833, Frederick began to build (but never completed) a frame house on his property. Because of failing health, he had to sell it. Captain George Lyman, after whom the street is presently named, purchased it in 1842. Frederick became postmaster in 1827 and moved the post office from Abel Dickenson's house on Diagonal Road to his house in the center of town.

As a township trustee, he improved the east–west road and spearheaded efforts to connect Wadsworth with Cleveland by building the north road (High Street), going through Sharon Center in the process. Unfortunately, the present Sharon Center was uninhabited at the time, but when it became somewhat "settled" by a few families, the road missed the present Sharon Center completely. It was not until many years later that the north road was curved west at Clark Corners to coincide with what is now the center of Sharon Center.

Finally, Frederick became an associate judge, so named to signify that he presided in the Wadsworth jurisdiction for the senior judge. He rode horseback to Medina to hear cases, and on his first case, he held court in a barn. (The Medina County Courthouse had not yet been erected.) When the sheriff called the litigants forward, no one moved: there were no litigants. Judge Brown had ridden the fifteen miles through the woods and thickets for nothing.

Historical accounts mention that John Brown was very close to his uncle—so much so that he spent as much time in Wadsworth as in his home in Hudson. People in Wadsworth considered him an honorary resident, if not a full-fledged one.

Early Business Center: Not a Mall Hangout

Since the Daniel Dean and Oliver Durham families set up camp at what is now Western Star, it follows that the first store would be in Western Star. In the mid-1820s, Henry E. Morgan opened a small store, believed to be situated on the southeast corner of what is now South Medina Line Road and Greenwich Road (Broad Street). Customers were few, commodities were hard to transport, people had little money, needs were basic, families preserved whatever they grew, game animals were abundant and few people knew that the store existed. It closed shortly after it opened.

Allen and John Pardee had other thoughts. In 1826, they opened a small store east of the center of Wadsworth at what is now the corner of Fairlawn and Broad Streets. The store flourished, mainly because more people lived in or near the center and because the Pardee brothers had closer ties with the villagers. The store soon outgrew itself, so Allen and John built a stone store on the southwest corner of the square, facing what is now College Street and behind what is now First Merit Bank. It became known as the "Stone Store," and later, because of age and other stores being erected, the "Old Stone Store."

Travel to the center of the village was difficult and somewhat treacherous. In 1830, Allen built a hotel on the opposite side of the east–west road for travelers on their way to points west or for customers who would not want to start their long journeys home on the same day that they came to purchase goods from the store.

The National Hotel, as it was usually known, was a two-story wooden building with a wraparound porch on two sides and a balcony on the second floor, also with a similar wraparound porch on two sides. Because Butt's Tavern was housed inside the hotel, those names—Butt's Tavern and the National Hotel—were almost interchangeable. Of note is that the National Hotel was only the third wooden structure in the center of the square.

Harvey Buell Spelman also ran a store in the center. His contribution as a storekeeper was not particularly significant, but the fact that he was the father of Laura Spelman, the wife of John D. Rockefeller Sr., made him a significant player in Wadsworth history. Laura was born in Wadsworth and lived on the east side of Main Street, where Main Street and School Drive intersect. (Laura was born on September 9, 1839, in the twenty-fifth year of Wadsworth's founding. In the late twentieth century, the house in which she was born was demolished to make room for a parking lot. One of Laura Rockefeller's great-grandsons came to Wadsworth during the 1989 175th anniversary celebration to see the house in which the matriarch was born, but it was no longer there.)

It should be noted that, while these stores were in the "center" of the village, they really were not. The geographical center of the five-mile square was about a mile west of the "center," where Isham School is located. It is unclear why the "center" was moved off-center; however, there seems to be evidence to support two possibilities that geography played a role in the misalignment: the road had not been cut through the densely wooded

Early stores on Main Street.

area where the center should have been, and the actual "center" was considerably lower than the high ground of the new "center" and was subject to voluminous water runoff. It also sloped west and south, making it difficult to lay out a flat and symmetrical square, particularly since there was a rise to the east as well. There is no documented evidence for this theory; however, word-of-mouth accounts for the location of the present center have long been spoken in Wadsworth by the old-timers.

From the first store at Western Star to the smattering of stores in the years following, little happened. It was not until the railroad came through Wadsworth in the mid-eighteenth century that the business district on Main, High, Broad and College Streets began to develop its footprints. While the early shops carried only essentials, the more "modern" shops carried comfort goods and more diversified commodities. Comfort goods included cigars and tobacco, dry goods for fancier clothing, jewelry and furniture. Added to the essentials were pharmaceuticals, wider arrays of food items and hardware and tools. The stores encouraged more trade, and more trade resulted in more and varied goods.

When the coal mines became king in Wadsworth, the "center" was flooded with workers who had need for entertainment as well as goods. Much of the entertainment revolved around "partaking of the grapes"; hence, the rise in the number of saloons and eateries.

THE PARDEE BROTHERS: FROM STORE TO MORE

Caroline Pardee was the last of the Pardees to be buried in Wadsworth as of this writing. She died on August 26, 2003, in her home at 161 Union Street, Akron, Ohio, where she was born and lived her entire life. She served as secretary and administrative assistant to the president of the university from 1953 to 1981. This writer was personally acquainted with her for over thirty years in his various capacities at the university. A portion of the Pardee history in this section was derived from the many conversations the writer had with Caroline over the years about her family.

Aaron Pardee was born on October 8, 1808, and had five sons with his wife, Eveline Blanch Eyles: William Eyles, Henry Clay, Don Albert, George Kendrick and Lionel S. There were also three daughters: Frances, the firstborn of the children, Almira and Ella. All five sons were attorneys, as was Aaron himself. Little is written about the girls except to cite whom they married.

From about 1842, when Aaron Pardee succeeded Frederick Brown as judge, and continuing until his death in 1898 at almost ninety years of age, the Pardees were probably the most prominent and powerful people in the village. Aaron's brothers, John and Allen, began the legacy by opening the first store within the village. Aaron continued the legacy by being the only practicing attorney until the mid-1880s. He became the first mayor of Wadsworth after the village was incorporated in 1866. In addition to being a storekeeper, Aaron's older brother, Allen, was an associate judge of Medina County, and Aaron's father-in-law, William Eyles, was justice of the peace, Medina County commissioner, state representative and an associate judge. In all, the Pardee family and their extended family guided Wadsworth through the pioneer days and years following.

Dr. George Pardee was only twenty years old when he began to practice medicine in Wadsworth, after "reading" medicine for a prescribed period of time. He was instrumental in founding the eight-doctor Medina County Medical Lyceum, a forerunner of the Medina County Medical Society. He used the upper floor of his brothers' Old Stone Store as his "medical school" but soon outgrew it and built a brick building on the northeast corner of Broad and Lyman Streets in 1845. Published stories in the *Enterprise*, the newspaper of the day, reported that Dr. Pardee's medical students robbed bodies from graves to facilitate their study of anatomy. George died in 1849, shortly before the new "hospital" was completed. Five Wadsworth doctors were educated at Dr. Pardee's medical school: Dr. C.N. Lyman, Dr. A.G. Willey, Dr. John Brown, Dr. Hanson Hard and Dr. William W. Beach.

Aaron Pardee, early settler and first mayor of Wadsworth.

In addition to medicine, Dr. Pardee was community-minded. He gave "community college" courses to the village residents on chemistry and was instrumental in founding the Wadsworth Academy (discussed later in this book).

Dr. Lyman is important in Wadsworth history, not only because he was a physician, but also because he was a *tireless* physician who cured the sick when cholera broke out during the construction of the Ohio-Erie Canal east of Wadsworth. Physicians were few during the epidemic and Dr. Lyman worked without rest as long as his body would permit. He was singled out for all his good work when President McKinley delivered a speech while standing on the steps of his home, also the location of his "hospital."

Don Albert Pardee was a highly educated man, a military man (he achieved the rank of brigadier general), an attorney and a war hero. He practiced law in Louisiana after being mustered from the military and then returned to Wadsworth after his retirement from law. His boyhood relationships with cousins, brothers and family members fostered his passion for Wadsworth. He memorialized this love for the village by building Vacation Ridge, an expansive seventeen-room home on Stony Ridge Road (now Reimer Road) that was poised high on the craggy ridge from which one could view the entire village of Wadsworth. He brought with him more than twenty Negro servants from Louisiana, one of whom was his personal valet. Don Albert could be seen riding a white horse into town, led by one of the servants bedecked in a top hat, to pick up mail. Other servants worked in the house and on the six farms that ultimately comprised the expansive landholdings that Don Albert amassed. The home still stands; however, it has been cut apart and made into two or more dwellings.

Stony Ridge Road was called thus because of a huge stone formation that prohibited the road from going straight. Instead, the road had to bend to the south and go in front of Vacation Ridge, causing travelers to go by the home on their way either direction. In the early 1930s, the Works Progress Administration (WPA) cut through the rock, straightening the road and taking away the close-up vantage point that travelers had of viewing the house. In the 1940s, the house was sold and broken into parts for single-use dwellings.

The Pardees have a designated plot in Woodlawn Cemetery, where Caroline was buried on August 29, 2003.

PARDEE MANSION ON WATRUSA: A "NAIL-BIDING" TIME

Walking down Watrusa Avenue today is not so impressive as it would have been 165 years ago, when the Pardee mansion was the focal point. Built on College Street but set back from the road, the house was impressive for the time, since many houses were made of logs or even of "green" lumber that did not present themselves as finished products.

The Pardee mansion, as it was called, was not really massive. It was a two-story wooden home that had three upstairs windows in the front and a wraparound porch that almost dwarfed the rest of the house.

Craftsmanship was said to be of the finest quality. The wood was oak, hickory and walnut from the local forests, the furnishings were of high quality and the amenities were avant-garde for the times. Wood was sawn and dried before it was used on the house, a process that was not always followed since drying was time-consuming and there were few places where it was done.

As was customary at the time, fruit trees sufficed as shade trees on properties, and few ornamental trees ever adorned the lawns and gardens. The Pardees had an orchard on the side of the house and a tennis court in front of the house.

Most members of the Pardee family lived close by, some as close as across the east–west road where St. Mark's Episcopal Church now stands on College Street. Recreation was never an "away" event; it centered on the homesteads. So it was with the Pardees, thus the reason for the tennis court.

In 1924, the Pardee mansion was moved to make room for some stores along the south side of College Street and west of what is now Watrusa Avenue. For many years prior to that, Caroline Pardee, the great-granddaughter of Aaron Pardee and daughter of Judge John Pardee, visited the home and shared reflections of the splendor that was built into the house. She had vivid images of the house as seen through the eyes of a child and, later, a young girl. She was always impressed by the stories that her father and grandfather recounted about notable people visiting the house (and, by extension, Wadsworth)—people who were very influential in the county, state and nation.

When the house was moved, it lost its charm. It was transformed into at least two houses. Nonetheless, the same wood that was nailed to the frame of the mansion then still exists today, 165 years later. This is of significance in that it was not the lack of sawn and dried lumber that impaired the building progress, but the fact that they had to wait for enough nails to be made

The Pardee mansion.

before they could finish it. In those days, nails were hammered out by hand in a blacksmith shop, a slow and laborious task. Caroline remembered stories about there being only seventeen nails anywhere in the county. Several blacksmiths had to be engaged to make the nails needed before carpenters could proceed with their work.

From 1838, when the mansion was started, until after Vacation Ridge was built, the Pardee families had the corner on elegant housing. It was several years before any house in Wadsworth exceeded the grandeur of their private dwelling.

THE EARLY BLACKSMITHS: RED-HOT CRAFTSMEN

The first account of any blacksmith working in Wadsworth was that of Hiram C. Kingsbury in 1819. He had a blacksmith shop on the bank of the brook east of the village. The word "brook" was used in other descriptions and probably meant the stream that began just south of Route 261, running south and slightly west through Durling Park and then alongside Sacred Heart School, emptying into the stream going from west to east in south Wadsworth.

Kingsbury was also said to be a traveling shoemaker and a tailor. He took his trades from house to house in a practice called "whipping the cat." (There seems to be no explanation for this term in any of the historical writings; however, the term dates back three hundred years and was usually attributed to tailors who went from house to house to sew for customers.)

Although blacksmiths were usually associated with making horseshoes, nails and other metal objects, some of the earlier ones made axes, the mainstay of tools for pioneer men. Peter Waltz was considered one of the first and most outstanding axe makers in the village. His shop was near where the High Church stands at the far southeast end of the township on Eastern and South Medina Line Roads.

Elisha Hinsdale had been a manufacturer of axes and scythes in Connecticut and brought his trade with him when he came to Wadsworth. The Hinsdale name will be prominent in sections devoted to education later in this book.

The blacksmith trade was key to nearly all other trades since most of the tools used in those industries were made by blacksmiths. Coopers, wheelwrights, tanners, carpenters, harness makers and wagon makers all used tools made by blacksmiths.

Perry Winkleman's blacksmith shop, one of the last in Wadsworth.

Perry Winkleman was the last blacksmith in Wadsworth and his shop functioned until the 1940s. He operated in a building built in 1868, and when Wadsworth City Hall was built in 1936, the building was razed. He worked for a time in the alley in the northeast corner of the square and, according to historical accounts, moved his shop to his home even later.

While Perry Winkleman did not work in the same way that earlier blacksmiths did in making tools, axes and nails, his skill was utilized by local farmers who needed repairs on their tools and equipment, especially in brazing metal, a process akin to welding.

Since the last blacksmith shop closed over sixty years ago, present readers will probably not know what they did or anything about their primitive machinery. The tools were simple: a forge for heating metal; tongs to hold the hot metal for shaping; and a hammer for beating the metal into shapes. Heat from the burning coals was intensified by forcing air into the forge. At first, bellows were used for forced air. Later, fans run by electricity or by hand forced air into the burning coals. When the metal was hot enough, the blacksmith would hit it with an appropriately shaped hammer while holding the piece with a tong. Horseshoes, tools and even cannons were made by blacksmiths.

HOTELS FOR A SMALL TOWN: ADJOINING BATH OUTSIDE

Hotels were in great demand during Wadsworth's early days. Travel was difficult, even from nearby settlements. It was not until roads were actually constructed on the pathways carved out of the dense woods that travel became a bit more palatable. Accounts were replete with stories of stumps still standing in the roadways, underbrush intertwined beneath the trees and mud so thick that travel was challenging if not impossible at times.

There were several activities that generated the need for hotels. A trip into Wadsworth from an outlying area to buy goods was a daylong event, especially during winter months, when shortened daylight hours placed an additional burden on customers. To overcome the difficulty darkness that presented, they would stay overnight before returning home the next morning. Settlers traveling through the village from the eastern states to points west could travel only a few miles a day and would need to find lodging before continuing. Men who came by themselves to find land for their families "back home" needed places to stay. Finally, entrepreneurs who were in the business of selling off acreages but never settled here also made good use of hotels.

In lieu of formalized hotels, some newly arrived families boarded other newer arrivals without charge or in exchange for work. However, as the population increased, hotels became more of a necessity than they had been earlier.

Hotels were not what the imagination conjures when we hear the word now. Instead, they were usually someone's house or a small outbuilding serving as a place to sleep. Most of these makeshift inns provided only a room, perhaps a place to eat, a bathtub and a shelter for horses. None had indoor plumbing. The "adjoining bathroom" was on the property adjoining the house—outside! Oftentimes, strangers shared rooms. There were no amenities as we know of them today and certainly no room service, except for a change of bedding when the person left…usually.

The Pardees had one of the first hotels but not *the* first, since their hotel did not open until 1830. The National Hotel, as the Pardee hotel was know, stood as an icon of the first "real" hotel, however. The Baughman House became a favorite place to stay in 1875 after the National Hotel burned to the ground the same year. (Those who remember the fire, as recorded in Reverend Brown's accounts, were stupefied to witness men using dynamite to blow up the raging inferno. The village "firemen" thought they had to do this to extinguish *what* was burning, the wood, so that there would be nothing left to burn.)

The Baughman House was located on the northeast corner of the square, just north of where the East Park now stands. Seth Baughman actually built the hotel, but he rented it to Noah Rasor, who changed the name, and it became the Rasor House for many years. Finally, it became the Park Hotel, but not the Park Hotel recognized by present-day Wadsworth residents, who remember the latter one that was part of the downtown during the first part of the twentieth century.

Across the street and north of the Myers Block, on the northwest corner of the square, stood the Kreider Hotel, where Ritzman Pharmacy and Holmesbrook Hardware are located now. The Kreider Hotel, built by John Kreider in 1894, was owned by the Kreider family, whose several descendants still live in Wadsworth. The original hotel was a wooden structure that burned down in 1904. It was replaced with a brick building with several rooms, a large lobby and a kitchen for guests. Next to the hotel was the home of Dr. W.C. Kreider, a well-known veterinarian, especially for equine and bovine animals. Dr. Kreider also had a livery stable behind the house that catered to people who came through Wadsworth on horseback. In an interview with

The National Hotel, a luxury for the time.

Mary Louise (Abott) Kuder, this writer learned that she rode her horse to school and left it at Dr. Kreider's stable during the day. At the end of the day, she would pick up the horse and ride to her home on Stony Ridge Road (now Reimer Road). Since Mrs. Kuder was born close to the turn of the century, her experience would have occurred prior to 1920.

The Park Hotel changed hands several times after the Kreider family owned it. The hotel was razed in the mid-1950s, when the present structure was built. It was not until about twenty-five years later that Wadsworth had another hotel.

THE SHEEPSHED: PIONEER ANSWER TO AN INSIDE MALL

The business district began to grow significantly fifty years after the first settlers arrived in Wadsworth, and stores became larger, types of businesses varied and the people became less concerned with survival and more attuned to the lighter aspects of life.

Where the Myers block stands today, on the northwest corner of the square, stood the Sheepshed. Were this building to be built today, it probably would not have had that name, since people would hardly know what a sheepshed looked like. It was a squarish building with an overhang, similar to the low-slung buildings that housed sheep during the times when sheep were commonplace in Wadsworth. Inside were several shops, the Home Restaurant, Otto Harp's Bakery, Uncle Bill's Saloon (operated by Mr. Robinson), the *Wadsworth News* office (not to be confused with the *Wadsworth News* that emerged years later) and Jay Bissell's barbershop.

The Sheepshed was a gathering place for the town gentry—some to drink, some to be shorn and some to eat. Still others came to read the paper or to report news that they had for the local paper.

The Home Restaurant also catered to travelers and to those living in rooming houses. The hotels had their own restaurants; however, on occasion, the "cook"—usually the wife of the owner—was unable to cook because of illness, and guests were sent to the restaurant in the Sheepshed.

Otto Harp's Bakery used wood-burning stoves for baking bread and pies. It catered to travelers and those staying at hotels more than to those who were permanent residents. In some cases, the rooming houses and some of the restaurants would use its baked goods.

Uncle Bill's Saloon was extremely popular and cause for much fraternization—some cordial and some not cordial. Especially after the coal

The Sheepshed, housing five enterprises, including the *Enterprise*.

mines began to increase in number, miners congregated at the saloons, and invariably, fights would break out. The town constable was usually alone at night and had to call upon Samaritans to help quell the frays.

Most popular of all was Jay Bissell's barbershop. Jay was known to be a practical joker and a hearty fellow. He reveled in taking advantage of newcomers to Wadsworth—either those passing through or those from nearby settlements—to encourage them to his side with charm and then making them the butt of his jokes. (Visitor: "What's that corral for?" Jay: "For jackasses; jump right in.")

Just as the name implies, the *Wadsworth News* reported just that. There is some evidence that it reached out to places such as Sharon Township and Norton Township but usually reported only what was happening in Wadsworth. There are accounts of horse thievery, cows "coming fresh" (giving birth), hogs being slaughtered, price of eggs, etc. The paper did not flourish nor did it have a long life.

The Sheepshed was replaced by the Myers block in 1905. Workers set up their construction site in the north park and began construction in 1904, finishing in 1905. Since that time, the block has been filled with dry goods stores (such as Wright's Department Store, Tubbesings), office supply stores, hardware stores, electric appliance stores, an art store, a saloon and, upstairs, a bowling alley.

THE BUGGY WORKS

Wadsworth was hardly known as the Detroit of buggy manufacturing, but percentage-wise, it had more buggy makers and shops than any other small settlement or village for miles around.

Augustus Phelps was the first to manufacture buggies. His buggies were rudimentary and functional, albeit solidly built and meant for the rough roads they traveled. He had a woodworker to build the body, a wheelwright to fashion the wheels and an upholsterer to make the seats—usually a piece of wood covered with leather. He was all three.

In 1838, George Beach and H.J. Traver established the first production buggy shop immediately north of where Grace Lutheran Church now stands. The business lasted until 1915 under a variety of names: Traver Company, Stevenson, Browning, Steele, Browning and Steele and R. Stevenson and Company. The company was so successful that it was able to ship buggies and carriages to distant communities, as well as to supply them for local sale.

When the average home was only less than five hundred square feet (as compared to present-day homes that are from twelve hundred to three or four thousand square feet), a building that was seven thousand square feet was extraordinary. Such was the size of what was Wadsworth's largest "manufacturing" structure in 1838 and years following.

A typical buggy shop in Wadsworth.

The Stevenson Buggy Works, one of several in Wadsworth in the 1800s.

The Stevenson name on a buggy was tantamount to having the name of a luxury car in today's idiom. One of the features that the Stevenson buggy boasted was ease of operation. This did not mean the buggy had "bells and whistles." Instead, it meant that the axle and wheel hub were of such a superior quality that the wheels turned with ease, permitting the carriage to move effortlessly. Given that this was before the days of metal bearings, such a claim was of some significance.

H.J. Traver has another reason for being important in Wadsworth history. He built a house across the street from his carriage shop that is now the museum for the Wadsworth Area Historical Society. Built in 1850, it housed three doctors after he lived in it. It is presently called the Traver-Johnson House, named after Traver, who built it, and Dr. Robert Johnson, a physician and early mayor, who lived in it. Dr. Johnson's daughter, Dr. Myra Johnson, used the house for her practice until she retired and lived there until her death. (The City of Wadsworth purchased the house, and in 2000, the historical society arranged to have the house dedicated to preserving Wadsworth history. Volunteers completely prepared the house for occupancy, and it now stands as a jewel containing over 190 years of Wadsworth memories.)

The second wagon works was on Broad Street, where NAPA Auto Parts is presently located. Captain Edward Andrews opened the shop in 1865 and employed ten men. He died in 1867. After Andrews's death, his brother, Josiah, took over the business and added carriages to his line of buggies.

Still later, the shop was operated by B.A. Long and J.S. Hougland. Following their ownership of it, wagon makers and blacksmiths Edward Bissell and W.H. Hanson continued manufacturing buggies and carriages on the site.

The need for buggies was still high in the latter part of the nineteenth century. To answer the demand, C.B. and Lloyd Wertz opened the third large carriage shop in Mills Street, immediately behind the last store on Main Street before it intersects with Mill Street. The shop opened in 1891 and limped into its demise as automobiles became more popular. The building remained, however, and it became Plank Elevator for many years. The building was later demolished and replaced with a parking lot.

PIONEER MILLS: ON THE CUTTING EDGE

The History of Medina County indicates that the first grinding of grain was done at Norton's mill, later called Tallmadge Village and, later still, Middlebury. All of these are in the Akron area. The Wetmore mill in Stow (at that time spelled *Stowe*) and Northampton mill (northwest of present-day Cuyahoga Falls) also played an important role in grinding various grains. It is apparent that these mills were the only ones in operation, given the fact that people coming from western settlements, such as Sullivan, Huntington and Wellington—several miles west of Wadsworth—would lay over in Wadsworth on their way to the mills.

Luther Hemingway built the first log-sawing mill in Wadsworth in 1819 on what is now Wadsworth Road, about a mile west of the square. At that time, it was called the Diagonal Road, since it went at a northwest angle from the east–west road, now College Street. It is not known why Hemingway would have built his mill there, since it was a good distance from the center of activity. There is an assumption that the nearby stream had enough force to power the circular saws and that it was conveniently located next to the mill.

Corn, wheat, rye, oats and barley—the grains of the time—were ones that sustained life. While some of the early pioneers ground it by hand using stones to crush the grains, they soon yearned for the types of mills that were extant in their home states—Connecticut, Vermont, New York and even Pennsylvania. Allen and John Pardee answered this need and built the first gristmill in the southwest side of the village, approximately one-half mile west and south of the intersection of Main and State Streets. They built their mill at that location to take advantage of the strong water flow available to turn the extremely heavy millstones. So perfect was the water flow that several other gristmills grew up close to the Pardee mill.

Sawmills had to be built near streams that provided power to the machinery as well. For this reason, sawmills were spaced throughout the village so long as there was water to turn the machinery. Joseph Loomis and son, Sheman, and Abel Beach and his son, George, built the first sawmill in 1824–25 on Blocker's Run (no longer a known name to present-day Wadsworth residents), located about a quarter mile from Main Street, close to the railroad tracks. This mill took two years to start because one day before it was to have opened in 1824, a strong rain swelled Blocker's Run waters and washed away the dam that was built to control the flow of water to the water wheel.

Captain George Lyman and Cyrus Curtis built their sawmill on Holmes Brook, about a mile west of the center and somewhat close to where Hemingway built his log-sawing mill. Holmes Brook had a strong current, giving the new mill a decided advantage.

In 1829, Jacob Long built his mill southwest of the Pardee and the Loomis-Beach mills. In all, there were at least four known sawmills located in the village. Prior to the establishment of the mills, boards were cut by hand, a time-intensive, difficult and ineffective way to prepare lumber for building houses. The advent of the mills made building easier. As a result, more houses were built to replace the log cabins that functioned as the earliest abodes.

The Pioneer Mill on State Street. *Courtesy of the Ralph Copley collection.*

It comes as an oddity—for a population that depended on the earth to feed it and work to reap what fed it—that rye, a substantial grain grown in the area because of its hardiness, was reserved for whiskey, not food, since the price from distillers was greater than that given by bakers. Barley was used as a staple in home cooking; corn was used for breads, animal food and curing certain respiratory ailments; and oat was used for human and animal foods. But rye—just whiskey.

ERASTUS LOOMIS: TURNED BLACK COAL GREEN

Erastus Gaylord Loomis became one of Wadsworth's most notable coal and lumber barons of the day; however, his name has not been a household word for several decades, probably a result of the demise of coal mines in Wadsworth.

Born in 1824, the son of schoolteachers Sherman and Lodemia Sackett Loomis, he was reared with a wealth of educational opportunities but hardly any financial ones. Both parents were community leaders, but as a result of being in a profession that did not command high salaries, Erastus was reared with handouts and hand-me-downs—all from a community that sometimes paid its teachers with goods and food rather than money.

Erastus determined that he would not live a life of poverty as his parents had. He saw that the Pardee brothers were successful because they were merchants instead of educators, and he sought to follow their paths instead of teaching. He was able to convince the Pardee brothers to hire him as a clerk. He thrived in business, despite having to take much taunting for speaking a highly refined English, a product of early mandates from his parents.

Erastus was so successful that he and his brother, Edgar, became partners in the Pardee store, and in 1858, at age thirty-four, he and Edgar purchased the building on the southeast corner of the square and made it into a mercantile business. Later, they sold the store to Daykin and Woodward, who operated it while the Loomis brothers were in search of even higher adventures.

The railroad had come through Wadsworth only a few years before, and Erastus saw an opportunity that almost no one else dreamed of pursuing. He noticed the area in Silver Creek, a settlement in the far southeast corner of Tract 1, was considerably lower than where Wadsworth Center was located. He had heard others talking about the pieces of coal that were on the ground next to the creek (Silver Creek) and thought they might be precursors to what might be beneath the ground.

With a vision that would change Wadsworth and make it into a booming coal mining town, he purchased the land and began digging. He had heard that people in Doylestown, about three miles south, had dug and found coal. Doylestown is much higher in elevation than Silver Creek and coal is usually in a vein that runs somewhat on a level path. He reasoned that the coal vein would be closer to the ground at the Silver Creek elevation than in Doylestown, and he began digging. To his amazement, he found that the coal was almost at ground level and all he had to do was dig north toward higher ground and, therefore, would not have to dig down.

The shaft mine at Silver Creek was born. Coal was abundant—so abundant that there seemed to be enough for local use and use elsewhere. The railroad was only several hundred feet from the opening of the mine, so he built the Silver Creek Railroad to connect with the Atlantic and Great Western Railroad and shipped the coal to distant places.

He next reasoned that if coal mining became a booming industry, it would be necessary to import people to mine the coal. More people meant more houses. The area where the Silver Creek mine was located was covered with a thick growth of oak, maple, cherry, hickory, walnut, chestnut and other hardwoods. Building implied the need for wood, bricks and carpenters. He began manufacturing bricks, probably on what was the Yockee farm, about a quarter of a mile north of the mine. He then formed Wise, Loomis and Company to build houses, using lumber from the four hundred acres of wooded land that he now owned, bricks from his brick-manufacturing business and carpenters whom he employed.

After the death of his brother Edgar in 1870, Erastus continued his partnership with Wise and purchased over three thousand acres of pine lands in Michigan. Mr. Wise was sent to run the operation and was so successful that he laid out a plan to build a village on the acreage. To this day, the village is known as Loomis, Michigan, named after Erastus Loomis.

Loomis's outreach was insatiable. He and Wise purchased 2,200 acres of pine in Missouri and built a mill there as they had done in Michigan.

The Silver Creek Railroad brought the mine so much success that he was called upon to become a director of the Lake Shore and Tuscarawas Valley Railroad (now part of the Baltimore and Ohio Railroad that runs south of Wadsworth), the CL&W Railroad and the CM&W Railroad. Later, he became president of the Cambridge Consolidated Coal Company of Columbus and the Akron Coal Company.

Loomis amassed an abundance of money, so much that he wielded more power than almost anyone else in Wadsworth for years after his initial successes. He built the first three-story building in Wadsworth, the

Left: Erastus Loomis—coal, lumber and building baron.

Below: The IOOF Building, the first three-story commercial building in Wadsworth.

International Order of Odd Fellows (IOOF) Building on the west side of Main Street in the middle of the block; the Agricultural Machine Shops; and the town hall. He was a major contributor to building the old Union School. His home at 302 Main Street was identified by the *Akron Beacon* in 1874 as having spacious parlors, an indication of its magnificence.

Indeed, the black, dusty, hard coal turned "green" for Erastus Loomis.

Coming of the Railroad: Full Steam Ahead for Wadsworth

Some thirty years after James Watt, the Scottish engineer who advanced the steam engine to power machinery—including the locomotive—trains began chugging through Wadsworth.

In 1850, Marvin Kent of Franklin Mills (now Kent, Ohio) had the dream of connecting New York City to St. Louis by rail. Despite realizing that this was a preposterous dream and that the legislature would not approve it, he started small by seeking to connect Warren, Ohio, to Franklin Mills, a distance of about thirty miles. He called the railroad the "Franklin and Warren" but noted in the charter that the road could be built anywhere in Ohio. He quickly changed the name to the Atlantic and Great Western Railway, with the thought in mind that such a grand-sounding name would fare better when he decided to expand his rail mileage.

Few people knew there was another railroad in Pennsylvania and New York by the same name. This railroad was making overtures to the Erie Railroad at Salamanca, New York, to connect with another railroad in Dayton, Ohio, the outcome of which would be a through route to St. Louis.

Kent approached the other railroad and struck an agreement with them to include his railroad for the venture. The newly formed railroad was indeed called the Atlantic and Great Western Railway Company, just as he had strategized when he gave his small venture the same name. Although the headquarters for the railway was in Meadville, Pennsylvania, Kent retained a seat on the board of directors as the Ohio representative.

Regulations for building railroads were in their infancy. As a result, there were many trial-and-error issues to overcome, particularly including the use of uniform rail gauges; building on various types of terrain; overcoming natural geological obstructions such as mountains and lakes; acquiring rights-of-way; transporting heavy machinery (that later would be transported by rail); and other problems, mostly unforeseen. The inability to solve the issues resulted in financial ruin for the company. Work stopped in 1858, a few years after the company organized the merger, but Kent was not to be discouraged. He sought financing from then unknown sources.

Europe was ahead of the United States in many areas, mainly because the nations of Europe were older and were not as involved in pioneer efforts. England was especially strong, so Kent and some other members of the board contacted James McHenry of London and other European investors for financing. With their money, the railway was completed.

In 1861, the Civil War broke out. Workers were hard to find since most of the men were in the military. Again, Kent was not deterred. He sent a contingent to Ireland to recruit laborers by offering them passage here and finding them homes. Wadsworth's Irish population emanated from that venture, as well as from the coal mining venture. Wadsworth's New England and Pennsylvania Dutch population was not pleased with this new element of its citizenry. Cultural, religious and ethnic problems festered for many years. Nonetheless, the work began to move forward and the railroad was ready to expand westward through Wadsworth.

James K. Durling, a prestigious Wadsworth leader who founded the first bank in Wadsworth in 1873 and was mayor from 1892 to 1894, plowed the first furrow for the extension of the railroad west of Kent and into Wadsworth.

It was a solemn occasion when the first train came through Wadsworth. The track was in the south end of the village and the "station" was a discarded boxcar. The entire town came out to watch the train. Flags were attached to every car on the train; the huge smokestack puffed billows of black smoke into the pristine farmland air; and the behemoth engine chugged laboriously through Wadsworth with regal majesty on its journey into the twentieth century.

This writer was acquainted with some whose parents witnessed the event. In addition to the description cited above, the most frequently told story was that no one in the village was drunk during this solemn event. Furthermore, no one was arrested for unsavory behavior and no one got hurt in the massive scramble to get as close to the train as possible. Ladies cried, men cheered and children screamed with unrestrained high-pitched glee.

There were some practical aspects of the event that are scarcely discussed in writing but were often mentioned during this writer's boyhood days. It seems that the station was to have been located at Western Star, about three miles east. Allegedly, five men went to the railroad officials and offered them a handsome sum of money to locate the station in Wadsworth. For whatever reason—probably the need for money—the offer was accepted and Western

The first railroad "station," an old boxcar.

Star lost out. A resident of Western Star, whose parents moved there from England in the late 1850s, recalled conversations that the loss of the railroad was the final blow that Wadsworth dealt Western Star, and for that reason, Western Star is only a crossroad now rather than *the* center of commerce that it had hoped to be.

Financial woes continued, even after the railroad was completed. The Atlantic and Great Western Railway Company fell into receivership, and in 1880 it was sold to the New York, Pennsylvania and Ohio Railroad Company, to be known as NYPANO. Meadville, Pennsylvania, lost its prominence when the main office was moved to Cleveland. In 1883, the Erie Railroad leased the tracks and operated under that name for seventy-three years, until it became the Erie-Lackawana Railroad on October 17, 1960.

The nearly one-thousand-mile road was the mainline from New York to Chicago, with spurs elsewhere. Of significance is that the very top of the steepest grade between the two cities is at the Silver Creek crossing on Silvercreek Road in Wadsworth. The climb from the east to Silvercreek Road is approximately seven miles. From that high point, it slopes an equal distance west through Rittman and beyond. The fact that the trains slowed almost to a stop as they labored up the long and steep grade from east to west and from west to east will be significant in the account to be discussed in a later chapter about the coal mining industry in Wadsworth.

A single track remains on the once busy railway. There are only two trains per week that travel the track, and then only to pick up materials from a factory in Wadsworth. This pales in comparison to the twenty-seven freight and two passenger trains that came through during the peak years of operation in the first quarter of the twentieth century.

PART II

COAL MINING TOWN: BURIED TREASURE

THE SILVER CREEK MINE

John Malaney, one of the string of people who owned the first mine in Wadsworth over a period of years and the writer's neighbor, recounted endless stories about the early mines. John closed the mine when a mule drowned in early 1936. Ironically, this mine was the first one to open in Wadsworth and the last major one to close.

This writer was present at the mine on the Saturday that it closed. Only he, his father and John Malaney were present that afternoon. It was a cold March day with the sun shining brightly through the only window, high toward the peak of the small shack that served as the mine office. The potbellied stove was raging warm with glowing coals that soon would die out and mark the end of the coal mining era in Wadsworth.

The writer's memory of John's stories and documented literature will serve as the backdrop for reporting the history of mines in Wadsworth.

Much has been said about the Ohio Companies (Ohio Injector, Ohio Match, Ohio Salt and Ohio Boxboard) being responsible for the industrialization in Wadsworth when they opened during the last whispers of the nineteenth century and the cacophonous clamor heralding the arrival of the new century. While no one will dispute the importance of these mechanized bastions in revolutionizing industry in Wadsworth, coal was the first real industry and the one that drove the increase in population, business and other industries.

Coal was mined in Wadsworth for local use in 1829, more than ten years before the first coal mine in Doylestown opened in 1840. Coal there was deep, since Doylestown sits on a high hill. Coal in Wadsworth was easy to access since Silver Creek (the creek, not the road), the location of the first mine, is one of the lowest points in the general area.

The area was completely covered with trees—almost all hardwoods. Lumberjacks working to fell trees for lumber would find evidence of coal on the ground near Silver Creek. They began collecting it and decided to see if any coal was located beneath the ground as well as on top of it.

According to John Malaney's accounts, men started digging into a gradual slope to the north and found that coal was close to the ground. They boasted that the vein was expansive and seemed to go in every direction, but the thickest one was to the north. The men dug in at an almost level line to the huge deposits of coal greeting them. They used timbers from the adjoining forest of hardwoods to support the shaft as they dug. Coal mines were born, and they prospered for about the next seventy years.

The reason the men were at that location in the first place was that they were cutting timber to sell to the railroad, since before 1869 locomotives used wood instead of coal for fuel. In a previous section, mention was made that Silver Creek Crossing was at the top of a seven-mile hill from the east and an equally long hill to the west, making it convenient for the trains to stop to pick up wood.

The terrain issue served for more than taking on wood alone. It would become a convenient stopping place for the coal to be loaded into the cars to be transported to places beyond. This gave the Silver Creek coal miners an advantage, since the distance from the mine to the tracks was relatively short, about fifteen hundred feet.

By 1869, the Wadsworth Coal Company (another one of the names given to the first coal mine) was furnishing coal to the locomotives, as well as shipping it, since the engines were then burning coal instead of wood. With the combination of these two outlets, the Wadsworth Coal Company began mining up to 150 tons of coal a day—all by hand with pick and shovel and loaded by hand onto small carts on tracks. It was at this time that Erastus Loomis built the Silver Creek Branch of the Atlantic and Great Western Railway to carry coal from the mine to the main track more quickly and efficiently.

Word that coal was abundant below Wadsworth spread, and in 1869, the Humphrey, Coleman and Company opened a mine. In 1871, the Myers Coal Bank opened on the opposite side of the village on what is now Reimer Road but was then Stony Ridge Road. The three mines would increase the labor force by about one hundred men, and these men would soon begin mining about forty thousand tons of coal a year—all by hand.

The coal mine story became a Wadsworth legend, so much so that *The Report of the Geological Survey of Ohio* for 1878 stated that over three-fourths of Wadsworth Township was located over a huge coal field. The only part of

Wadsworth that did not have a significant vein was the southwest portion of the township. The geological survey explored further and found that the vein under Wadsworth actually extended to Massillon, Ohio, a distance of about thirty miles. The configuration was somewhat long but narrow, starting in and around Massillon and traveling north-northwest to Wadsworth, ending almost at the end of the northern portion of Wadsworth Township. While it did extend east of Wadsworth for several miles, the thickness of the vein made it somewhat impractical to mine beyond the Wadsworth Township borders. Miners felt that it was not profitable to mine if the vein were only two feet thick or thinner.

Mine owners in the far northwest corner of the township saw how advantageous the southeast rail spur was and they constructed their own spur. This spur was more costly since the northwest mines were about three miles distant from the mainline in Silver Creek. The track went from the mainline, starting about a quarter of a mile west of Silvercreek Road, traveled north toward Sacred Heart Church on Broad Street, continued about a mile farther north and then turned west near Clark Corners and ended at the Hinsdale, Oberholtzer and Pardee mines, west of where the Great Oaks Shopping Center is now located.

The rail spur resulted in several additional mines opening in the northwest section of the township. Even the Silver Creek Mine (yet another name for the first mine) opened a second shaft in the vicinity of Hartman Road, north

A typical coal tipple used in all the mines.

of Route 261. It had already opened another mine at the end of Fairlawn Avenue in the vicinity of Durling Park. The Card and Barrett Coal Company of Cleveland saw the potential for great profits and opened one mine on the northwest section and one on the northeast section of the township. (O.V. Dibble was the mining engineer for the Card and Barrett Coal Company, later the Card and Prosser Coal Mining Companies, and had so much respect for Henry Card, one of the owners, that the Dibbles named their son Card Dibble. Card went by this name all his life, and Wadsworth residents thought that it was a nickname until the "secret" was revealed that Card was his real name.)

On August 24, 1882, the Excelsior Coal Company mine (a relative newcomer to Wadsworth from Akron) mined 1,201 tons of coal in a nine-hour day and loaded it into seventy-nine railroad cars—all by hand. This feat ranked as the largest tonnage of coal ever taken from a mine in northern Ohio in a single day. Researchers have tried to determine whether any other mine ever surpassed this record and concluded that none had.

LIFE OF THE MINER

The interior pathways in mines were about four feet high and about the same measure wide. Each miner had to dig his own shaft, extract his own coal, load the coal into a cart, blast for coal, bail out water and shore up his own mine. Since few men are four feet tall, they would need to lie on their stomachs or bend over the entire day to earn their dollar by the end of the day. If they were extra-industrious, they might earn a bit more. Miners called particularly low mines "pinch gut" mines.

Miners used lard oil for their lamps since kerosene was too smoky and would contaminate the air in the already oxygen-starved environments. Later, acetylene lamps became popular since they were brighter and cleaner. Still later, battery-operated lights were used, but they had limited use because the batteries would discharge quickly and were expensive. Large fans evacuated foul air from the mines, but they were not too effective. Overexposure to carbon monoxide was common and "bends" were a daily occurrence. It was not unheard of for men to die in the mines. Flooding was also a problem, since the water table was often at the level where the coal vein was located. Blasting usually occurred at the end of the day so the dust would settle before the morning shift began working. While blasting was faster in some ways, it had the potential to slow down the process since miners would have to break the huge boulders of coal into smaller pieces that were manageable for use.

The Great Coal Mine Strike

Beginning in the 1870s, coal miners were becoming more and more frustrated by the low wages they were receiving, particularly since they knew mine owners were making obscene profits from their backbreaking work. Petitions to the owners to raise wages were never heeded, so the men began putting stone into the mix of coal they sent to the mouth of the mine. The owners warned them about this, but despite repeated reprimands, the stones kept appearing. To counteract this, the owners built a heavy screen onto which the miners loaded their coal. Only the large chunks of coal would remain as smaller pieces of coal and rocks would fall to the ground. The miners were paid only for the coal that remained on the screen. This practice angered the men, so they went on strike.

Replacing the workers would be difficult since working in the mines was distasteful and almost inhumane. Local efforts to recruit miners failed. Owners enticed some Irish miners who had settled in the Doylestown area to work in the Rogues Hollow mines. These strikebreakers were not sufficient to provide the quantity of coal for the now voracious appetite to which buyers were accustomed; there was a need for more.

Erastus Loomis decided to go into Kentucky, West Virginia and Alabama to recruit Negroes for the mines. He was aware that this would cause a violent stir in Wadsworth, since not too many years earlier, New Englanders who sought to marry Pennsylvania Dutch were discouraged from intermarriage and considered to be in a "mixed marriage" if they did. By supposition, he reckoned that introducing Negroes would generate an even more inflammatory response.

His cunning prevailed. Instead of housing the Negroes in Wadsworth, he built a stockade in Hametown (south of Sherman and northeast of Doylestown) with posts from the Silver Creek trees. The Negroes lived there and were shuttled to the mines on the various railroad spurs now available. The stockade was self-contained, with a commissary and school, making any integration with the Wadsworth or Doylestown communities unnecessary. Even with all of these precautions, there were threats, hostilities and uprisings. Loomis called the governor and asked for the state militia to come to Hametown to protect the peace. After about six weeks, the furor died down and the militia returned home. The striking miners finally accepted the screening process and returned to work.

After the strike ended, all but about fifteen Negro families returned to their homes; the rest settled in Wadsworth. There are still descendants living in Wadsworth whose ancestors came to work in the mines.

The coming of the railroad, coupled with the mining operations, generated an explosive burst in population, new businesses, other industries, newspapers, schools and churches. According to the *Historical and Business Directory of Wadsworth* in 1870, there were seventy-five businesses and related professional services then operating in Wadsworth—this from only three or four forty years earlier. Indeed, the coal mining industry can claim the right of primacy for the beginning of growth in Wadsworth.

PART III

WADSWORTH CHURCHES: FAITH, BRICKS AND MORTAR

THE CONGREGATIONAL CHURCH

The church of the Puritan fathers was the Congregational Church. Since Wadsworth was in the Connecticut Western Reserve, the Congregational General Association of Connecticut and the General Assembly of the Presbyterian Church felt responsible for sending missionaries to this far reach of the Connecticut landholdings.

During the early days, both denominations were combined together. The Western Reserve Synod of the Presbyterian Church was expelled from the Presbyterian Church about 1852 because some of the locals were practicing liberal beliefs. After that, the church was called simply the Congregational Church.

The first Congregational church within the town center was built of logs and was the "official" church of the town. The fact that it was built by many hands in a short period of time was not the most noteworthy feature of its construction—doing so without whiskey was. This boast was not supported by all, however, since some decided not to assist unless whiskey was part of the church raising.

Charter members of the Congregational Church were Judge Frederick Brown and wife; Augustus Mills and wife, Martha Pettibone Mills; Captain George Lyman and wife, Ophelia Cook Lyman; Benjamin Agard; Sherman Loomis; and Jacob Lindley.

The Reverend Joseph H. Breck was the first to preach in Wadsworth in 1823. He also served at Harrisville (now Lodi) and alternated between the two congregations. The Reverend Amasa Jerome became the first pastor in 1826 and was installed in the new barn that Benjamin Agard had just built. The Reverend Gilbert Fay followed in 1830. He died in 1835 from an epidemic that gripped the town at the time. During his pastorate, the church membership increased from eleven to seventy members.

In 1829, the Congregational Society built a building measuring twenty-four by thirty-six feet. Twelve years later, it replaced the log church with a wooden one made of boards. This building remains to this day and is occupied by St. Mark's Episcopal Church. After the Congregationalists vacated the church, the building was sold to the First Mennonite Church and then to St. Mark's.

EPHRIAM HUNSBERGER

Wadsworth has three Mennonite churches—the older order Mennonites, of which there are two churches, and the First Mennonite Church, a more progressive branch of the Mennonite Church. In this instance, the "First" in First Mennonite does not denote primacy in arrival but is part of the sect's title.

Until 1851, only the older order Mennonites were part of the Wadsworth community. They were joined during that year by a more liberal group of Mennonites who came from Montgomery and Berks Counties in Pennsylvania. Only four of this sect migrated and began their lives west of Wadsworth, where other Mennonites lived. Jonas Nice, Henry Nice, John Alderfer and Jacob Oberholtzer and their families constituted the entire contingency of the "new" Mennonites, as they were sometimes called. Only Jacob Oberholtzer was not related to a Nice; Mrs. Alderfer was Katherine Nice before marriage.

The Reverend Ephriam Hunsberger came to Wadsworth with his father, Abraham Hunsberger, to visit the latter's sister. While here, Ephriam preached in various houses and developed a rapport with the "new" Mennonite families. Upon his return to Montgomery County, Pennsylvania, he received a call from the "new" group to come to Wadsworth to organize a liberal Mennonite Church here.

The Reverend John H. Oberholtzer, a leader of the liberal faction in Montgomery County, ordained Ephriam a bishop in 1852, making him eligible to serve the new congregation upon his return to Wadsworth.

Ephriam and Wadsworth were born in the same year, 1814. The son of a farmer and carriage maker, Ephriam learned both ways of making a living. Mennonite preachers were not paid in those days and, therefore, needed a trade for financial support. In addition to working as a carriage maker, Ephriam also farmed while here in Wadsworth.

Ephriam Hunsberger, Wadsworth's first new Mennonite preacher.

In the year following his arrival in Wadsworth, Ephriam was able to build a small frame church on Diagonal Road (now Wadsworth Road) with financial help from his church in Pennsylvania. Although vey small, the church was large enough to accommodate the few families who were members. They also established a Mennonite cemetery next to the church that is maintained to this day.

Ephriam's vitality engendered a great deal of credibility for the "new" church, as well as for himself. It is of note that shortly after he arrived, he was able to become an active member in the development movement of the General Conference of Mennonites of North America. Beyond that, he was instrumental in helping to make the Mennonite College a reality, the only one in the United States at the time. The evolution of the college will be treated in a separate section later in this book.

Although the first settlers in Wadsworth were from New England (and not German), and the Pennsylvania Dutch did not arrive until later, five churches were basically German in nature by 1860: two Mennonite congregations, two Lutheran and Reformed congregations and one Reformed congregation. German was spoken in all of these churches. By contrast, from 1814 to 1860, the New Englanders had established only three churches: Methodist, Congregational and Disciple. It is believed that the Reverend Ephriam Hunsberger was one of the motivating forces driving the migration from Pennsylvania to Ohio through his General Conference ties, the Mennonite College and his involvement in a factory that built sashes, doors and blinds. What had started out in about 1830 as a people who were not especially welcomed by the New Englanders seemingly empowered themselves by 1860—probably because Ephriam Hunsberger came to visit his aunt ten years earlier.

THE OLD MENNONITE CHURCH

When the first Mennonites came to Wadsworth from Pennsylvania and Canada, they settled west of Wadsworth Center and in part of Guilford Township. The ones from Canada were originally from Pennsylvania but, after the Revolutionary War in the 1780s, went to Canada for a variety of reasons, including the availability of expansive farmland and the personal freedom to practice their peace-loving faith as they wished.

Henry Geissinger, one of the ones who came from Canada, is credited with starting the Old Mennonite Society of Wadsworth and Guilford Townships. He was born in Northampton County, Pennsylvania, in 1786 and came to Wadsworth in 1825, just eleven years after the first settlers arrived. Geissinger went to Bucks County, Pennsylvania, with horse and wagon and moved William Overholt to Wadsworth to serve as the minister of the newly formed Mennonite Church.

In Anna Lois Rohrer's history, *Mennonites of Medina County*, she lists the names of some of the first Mennonite families arriving in Wadsworth: Philip

The Old Mennonite Church, built on Diagonal Road.

Geissinger and Daniel Wideman, from Pennsylvania; Nicholas and Samuel Kurtz, father and brother of Henry Geissinger's wife, Elizabeth; Abraham Beam; Samuel Nahrangang; Samuel and Elizabeth (Nahrangang) Kulp; and John Wideman, brother of Daniel, from Canada.

Over a period of only a few years, the number of Mennonites in Wadsworth numbered about one hundred, counting children. Most of the families were large, with six to twelve children. Many of the newcomers had come hundreds of miles from Pennsylvania and Maryland at great expense and travail. Their reason for coming was to build a new life of worship for themselves and for their children. To do this, they established their first church in 1832 on the southeast corner of Seville Road and Mennonite Road on the site of the present Maple Hill Church.

Jacob F. Leatherman of River Styx brought the first log for the first Mennonite meetinghouse in Medina County. The church was built of logs—as were houses—and was simply a room in which people could congregate to hear the word of God. The description of the interior of the church states that the preacher stood behind a desk that rested on the same level as the rest of the church and sat in a chair behind the desk. The reason for this arrangement was to manifest the belief that the clergy was ordained from the congregation and was not above any other person in the membership. Sitting in plain wooden benches also supported their Anabaptist belief that man is to live in a spirit of simplicity and frugality. German, or a dialect of German, was spoken during the service.

The congregation of Mennonites was not without controversy. In a previous section, the account of the First Mennonites suggested a variation in the approach to expressing their faith. This group felt a need for a more liberal expression, while the Old Mennonites adhered to the strict tenets of the original doctrine of their Anabaptist foundation. Even among the Old Mennonites, there were some differences that arose regarding the matter of having Sunday schools. The original group of Mennonite settlers took one view and other Mennonites another. When it came time to build another church to replace the fifty-five-year-old log cabin, rather than combine their efforts, one of the groups built the Bethel Mennonite Church a short distance west of Maple Hill Church. According to Anna Lois Rohrer's research, the controversy lasted about ten years. People in Wadsworth today are not aware of the conflict since the Mennonites sorted out all of their differences within their own ranks, typifying their strong foundation of Christian charity and understanding.

THE LUTHERAN CHURCH

As was stated in earlier accounts, a large proportion of the population of Wadsworth was of Germanic background, unlike the earliest settlers, whose heritage was predominantly English. So it was also with the churches. The Reformed Church had a strong German component, as did the Lutheran Church, founded a short time later.

The Reverend Dr. Hamilton, MD, a neighboring Lutheran minister, attempted to establish a congregation in Wadsworth in 1861, but the outbreak of the Civil War dampened his efforts. The Joint Synod of Ohio sent a student from Capitol University to make another attempt in 1869, but he, too, failed. It was not until 1882, when the Reverend Dr. J.C. Kauffman agreed to preach in Wadsworth, that the Lutheran Church in Wadsworth became a reality.

The first Lutheran church built in the city.

The first services were held in the Disciple Church, but the small congregation wanted its own church. Groundbreaking for the wooden structure occurred on May 11, 1885, coordinated by Reverend Kauffman himself. In addition to several items of religious symbolism placed in the copper box that was buried, the pastor thought to include a copy of the *Wadsworth Enterprise*, a local paper.

John Seiberling contributed $500 toward the purchase of the lot, which cost $1,400. John Seiberling was the father of Frank and Charles Seiberling, of rubber fame. The lot was purchased from Lauraette Pardee Jones, a relative of Judge Allen Pardee.

The church grew quickly, reaching 261 members by the turn of the century after starting with only 29 a few years earlier. On June 13, 1885,

Fred Slanker, a well driller with a long legacy of drilling wells in Wadsworth and surrounding areas, was baptized in conjunction with the first service held in the nearly finished church.

After Reverend Kauffman resigned, Reverend Dr. C.B. Etter succeeded him on January 1, 1895. Stories still abound about Etter's collapsing on the altar and dying near the end of the service that he was conducting on July 21, 1935.

THE METHODIST CHURCH

In the early settlement days, religious meetings were held in homes. As early as July 1814, Oliver Durham used his home to bring together other settlers such as the Deans, the Durhams and the Warners. Salman Warner visited the area to select a farm and was Dean's brother-in-law and Durham's father-in-law.

There was no Methodist minister. As a result, the prayer services were held together with people of other denominations, especially Congregationalists. The difference between the Methodist and Congregationalist styles of worship was pronounced, albeit workable. Worshipping together necessitated a compromise on the readings so the differences could be mollified.

In 1816, the Methodists left the "non-denominational" prayer meetings and started their own. Assembling first in the South School and moving to the North School after it was built, they convened a small group consisting of the Warners, Durhams, Wrights and Mrs. Polly Kirkum. As their numbers grew, they began alternating between the two schools to make it easier for people in the respective areas to attend, and they later included the west school on Diagonal Road for the same purpose.

The first minister was Lysander Hard, who came in 1818. There is no record of his having an official charge to preach here; nonetheless, he served the people well as an itinerant minister. The small congregation appreciated his preaching but wanted a minister who would lead them spiritually and administratively as well. They knew that they would need a permanent meeting place if they were to attract a resident minister.

In 1834, Levi Blakeslee sold a half acre of land on the north–south road (Main Street) to the Methodist Episcopal Society of Wadsworth for fifty dollars. Receiving the property in the name of the society were Chauncey Hart, Benjamin Tyler, Thomas Reese, Salman Warner, Abraham Betts, John Nesmith, Ambrose Cook, Matthew Borland and Dudley Griswold.

The first Methodist church in Wadsworth, built on the property adjacent to Central Middle School.

Lumber for the new meeting place came from Cyrus Hard's woods. Men carried the timber the short distance from the woods to the church property by way of a "logging bee," something akin to a PTA workday, where several parents assemble to make quick work of the task at hand. The wood was planed by hand since there were no planing mills, and the doors and windows were made by hand as well. The new building was thirty-six by forty-six feet, with the "audience room," pulpit and altar occupying the entire area. Different from the pulpit of the Mennonites, the one in the Methodist meetinghouse was elevated so the minister could see and be seen.

The Disciple Church

The Disciple Church that was built about 1860 still stands and is used for the congregation of the First Christian Church. Early preaching was supplied by itinerant ministers, and it was not until the 1860s that a pastor assumed the pulpit for the more than one hundred members.

The controversies regarding the New Englanders and the Pennsylvania Dutch were waning. Aaron Pardee, a staunch member of the New England group, was called upon to teach a Sunday school class in German at the Disciple Church, a benchmark in improved relations between the two factions. He learned German so he could communicate with his Pennsylvania Dutch clients in matters of law.

The Disciple Church was originally oriented with the altar on the west end of the church but was moved to the east end when major renovations were made to the then stark edifice. Other improvements included the installation of an organ, transforming windows from square to gothic, building a vestibule and adding a baptistry.

Early ministers were brothers John and James Encel, J.B. Knowles, F.M. Green, C.F. Cronemeyer and A.B. Williams. A host of others followed later. These ministers suffered through the depressed financial times of the 1880s but maintained the stability of the congregation nonetheless. Despite the ten-year financial drought, they prevailed through perseverance and commitment. As a result, the church continues and flourishes to this day.

The Disciple Church is said to have been the church of President James A. Garfield, since he attended and spoke there so many times. He and Burke A. Hinsdale, who will be discussed in the section under education, were close friends while Hinsdale was president of Hiram College and before.

THE EMANUEL CHURCH: THE HIGH CHURCH

Three years after the arrival of the first settlers, the High Church was the meeting place for bringing worshipping Lutherans and Reformed Christians together. This association lasted many years, until Lutherans and Reformed—both of German ancestry—went separate ways, doing so without controversy.

The High Church is located in Wayne County presently, was located in Medina County previously and before that was located in Summit County—within a radius of not more than a few hundred feet. It must be noted, however, that when the church was founded in 1817, all three of these counties were Portage County. Later, Portage County separated into the other two counties.

The High Church is viable to this day, with a legacy of ministering to a largely agrarian congregation. Its picturesque setting, high on a hill that slopes precipitously to the east, preserves the names of its early and recently deceased members in one of the areas oldest cemeteries.

Jerusalem Lutheran Church

Situated in the heart of the farming area where many of the Lutherans of German background settled, Jerusalem Lutheran Church (now called Acme Lutheran) continues to serve this community since its founding earlier in the nineteenth century. Lutheran and Reformed denominations were combined in the beginning, but Jerusalem became solely Lutheran during the 1880s.

One of the early pastors, the Reverend B.L. Westenbarger, was the grandfather of local resident Glen Westenbarger, who at the time of this writing is in his eighth decade of life.

Sacred Heart Church

The population of Wadsworth began to increase after the coal mines and railroad were introduced to the area. The railroad needed constant repair, and the coal mines needed a never-ending supply of men to replace the ones who would leave, become injured or even die. Most of the people remaining from the earlier settlers were either not willing to do this kind of work or were otherwise occupied and could not contribute to either railroad maintenance or mining.

As was mentioned in earlier accounts, miners were imported from Ireland. These people were usually Catholics but had no church in which to worship. In 1886, the first Roman Catholic church was built in Wadsworth on land donated by John Gallagher. The farmhouse in which Mass was celebrated was located on the site of the present Sacred Heart School. The size and shape of the house was such that the east end was actually large enough to accommodate the small group of Irish Catholics who came to work on the railroad three years earlier.

Mass was held only when a priest could come from distant locations such as Wellington, Medina, Doylestown and, on occasion, from cities even more distant. The new cast of players in the Wadsworth area was an anomaly and a source of friction, since this was the first time that people who were not Protestant surfaced in the solidly Methodist, Congregational, Baptist, Lutheran and Mennonite community.

The general population greeted the Catholics with disdain, a treatment that caused them to isolate themselves into geographical conclaves, usually in the vicinity of the mines or near the railroad. One family, the Hutchinsons, who had previously lived in Doylestown, moved to a dirt road parallel to

John Gallagher's home, where Sacred Heart Church began.

the tracks at the far end of the east–west road, now called Silvercrest Road. The several brothers, their families and offspring inhabited almost the entire end of the road, with only one or two other families interspersed. Some of the relatives, including the Malaneys, branched out along the main part of Silvercrest Road. Almost all worked in the mines.

The Catholic population began to increase when the Ohio Companies needed hundreds of employees. The Ohio Match Company alone needed over one thousand workers since all of the operations were done by hand. People from southern and eastern Europe began to arrive before the turn of the twentieth century and continued to do so into the 1920s. Fifty families came from Italy, mostly from Sicily, with only two from the mainland. Slovaks, Slovenians, Czechs, Hungarians and a few Polish also arrived. Nearly all of these were Catholics. As a result, the church had to enlarge.

The Gallagher house served as the church for several years, but in 1915, Joe Bender, an actor, restaurateur, landowner and devout Catholic, donated land east of the temporary church for a new and larger church. The congregation built a small wooden church and was served by Reverend John

Ryan, a part-time priest. It was not until 1923 that Sacred Heart had its first full-time pastor, Reverend C. Leo Brown.

There was no rectory for Father Brown, so he lived with parishioners until Joe Bender and Adam Haller purchased the Hiram Baughman house across the street from the church. Later still, Father Brown was able to purchase the William Everhard house immediately adjacent to the church for the rectory.

In 1929, the wooden church was moved to the side lot during construction of the brick structure. After the new church was built, the wooden structure was dismantled and rebuilt at the corner of Durling Drive and Broad Street.

The church proper has had two major additions since that time. Additionally, in 1949, Sacred Heart School was built and administered by the Vincentian Sisters of Charity from Bedford, Ohio. In 1957, the second story was added. Sacred Heart School was the first parochial school in Medina County. Land for the school was donated by Joseph and Katherine Bender, the same couple who donated land for the church forty years earlier.

First Baptist Church

When the coal miners struck in Wadsworth and the mine owners needed strikebreakers, the owners went south to bring in Negroes to work the mines. While many of the temporary miners returned to their homes following the end of the strike, some families stayed.

There were stories around Wadsworth that some churches actively kept the Negroes from worshipping with their congregations. As a result, the few remaining families opened their own church on the corner of Kyle and Mill Streets in 1880. While they resided within the walls of the stockade in Hametown, they worshipped there. With the stockade now dismantled, so was their church; hence, the need for a new one.

Rising Mount Zion Baptist Church, later renamed the First Baptist Church, recorded the following families in its membership: Mr. and Mrs. Phillip Scott, Lemuel Cheatham, Ned James, William Dyson, Pleas Harris, Robert Heath, Primus Watson, Alfred Early, William Stokes, Creed Haskins, Henry Benton, Beverly Mann, Royal Jones, Winfield Pollard, Richard Williams, Woody Coleman, William Branch, James Greene, Henry Taylor, Alexander Jones, Aurelius Howard and Meridith Clark. Those without mates were James Johnson, Paul Coleman, Amanda Greene, Leslie Pollard, Amelia Greene, Sally Miles and Millie Jones.

The lot on which the church is built was donated by Aaron Pardee, with financial assistance from Pastor J.C. Kauffman of Grace Lutheran Church, the Reverend S.C. Goss of Trinity Reformed Church and from other residents of Wadsworth.

Early ministers of the church were the Reverends J.J. Moore (minister at the stockade), Collins, J.W. Chetham, Joseph Spells, J.R. Greene, H.B. Brown, Paul Woolridge and Herban (no first name known).

PART IV

EDUCATION IN WADSWORTH: FROM BLEAK TO GREEK

THE EARLY SCHOOLS

The Connecticut Western Reserve lands were divided into sections, or townships. The sixteenth section of each township was dedicated to government, churches and schools. Although the first school was not in the sixteenth section, later schools were.

The people from Connecticut were strong on education, but they did not bring funding with them to start schools. This did not deter them, however. Three years after the first settlers came to the region, Miss Harriet Warner started a school in her father's double log cabin. This small space was soon outgrown, so the following year, 1818, the public underwrote the cost of a log schoolhouse on the east–west road (Broad Street) at the end of Hartman Road. Dr. Marcus Brown, son of Judge Frederick Brown, was the first teacher in what was called the South School. Following Marcus was his sister Catharine and, later, Mrs. Timothy Hudson.

This school was also quickly outgrown, and a second school, the North School, was built at the intersection of the upper end of Hartman Road near Route 261. One of the teachers of the school was Lodemia Sacket Loomis, who addressed the commencement class of 1887 and pointed out that the reason the school was not built in the sixteenth section was that the section was covered with trees and there were few people living there. She continued with a recitation of the pupils she had at the school: Eugene and Laurette Pardee (children of Judge Allen Pardee); Ann and Pardee Butler; George Weeks; Mary Ann and Eveline Eyles; and names she could not remember. Mrs. Loomis was eighty-nine years old when she recalled the beginnings of her teaching experience in Wadsworth.

The first schoolhouse in the village, located on Broad Street opposite Hartman Road.

As was stated in the opening of this book, the first settlers arrived on the east end of the township in what is now Western Star. Houses, although few, were scattered around that region and did not move into the center of the township until later. One of the teachers reported that students had to tramp through the woods and find their way to the school by marked trees and beaten paths. Not unlike present-day truths, it was thought that even if children did not learn the three courses taught—reading, writing and geography—they at least gave their mothers freedom to busy themselves with housekeeping chores.

There was no compulsory education in Ohio in the early part of the 1800s. Any schools that were in existence were called voluntary schools. Teachers were paid about $1.50 each week plus room and board. If money was not available, the teachers were paid with food and goods. Those paid with corn would take the corn to Middlebury (East Akron) and sell it to distillers, who made it into whiskey, translating food into money. Some teachers worked in the homes where they boarded, cutting trees or tilling the ground, and were paid by the owners.

After the advent of voluntary schools, a new school appeared in the center of the township. Dr. William Welton taught in a log house owned by Judge Frederick Brown circa 1820. Teachers were not required to be certified; however, only distinguished and tried intelligent people could teach. Captain George Lyman, Lemuel North, John Nesmith and Sherman Loomis followed Dr. Welton as teachers. From the Brown house, the school was moved to the first structure built to serve as a school in Bender's Court, immediately behind St. Mark's Episcopal Church, before 1826. While the exact date is not recorded, there is mention made that the Mormon apostle Joseph Smith spoke at the school in 1826.

Between 1829 and 1831, the township established twelve districts, with a one-room school in each district. Some of the original buildings still exist and are used for private dwellings. Notable among these are the Number One School on Wall Road, the Number Eleven School on Johnson Road (one quarter mile east on Silvercreek Road on the north side) and others scattered throughout the city.

The original school built on Bender's Court became too small and needed to be expanded or closed. Another option was to build another school that would house the growing number of children. The latter prevailed. The Long School, so called because of its length, was built on the north–south road (High Street) where the CVS parking lot is now located. The south one-third of the school was for smaller children, and the north two-thirds, for older ones. The "playground" was the Judge Allen Pardee woods behind the school or the front lawn of the Disciple Church across the road from the school. The Long School was abandoned in 1869 and replaced by the Union School, built on the site of the present Central Intermediate School.

The Union School

When the Long School became overcrowded, the students were housed in various building throughout the village; notably, the town hall, since it was not used during weekdays. This arrangement was unsatisfactory logistically and administratively, in that both buildings required additional financial support and personnel to house the students. It would be more efficient to have only one building large enough to accommodate all students.

In 1869, land was purchased from Isaac Griesmer and J.K. Durling (where the present Central Intermediate School is located) for $1,200. The architect

The Union School, built on the site of the present Intermediate School.

was the husband of the granddaughter of Philemon Kirkum, a prominent member of the village and a Revolutionary War veteran.

Union School was Wadsworth's first multistoried school building, boasting three floors. The first two floors were for classrooms and the entire third floor was dedicated to open space for community assemblies and other large-group activities. When the lower two floors became overcrowded, the third floor was partitioned into classrooms to accept the increased enrollment.

The school opened on November 14, 1870, with board of education members serving as hosts: Aaron Pardee, J.W. Daykin, James K. Pardee, J.S. Houston, E.G. Loomis, E.K. Kremer and J.D. Ross, clerk. Marion C. Lytle was the superintendent and a teacher. Loisa Hinsdale, Sadie Lytle and Hettie McDougall were teachers with specific assignments in their area of teaching.

Throughout this entire period, the same names appear as leaders. Some of them were educated and/or held prestigious positions; some were successful business owners; and others were leaders in other venues. Erastus Loomis, the coal mine, lumber and construction baron, is said to have either contributed heavily or gave the entire $25,000 cost of the school. The school was demolished in 1907 to make room for the then new brick building that still stands with its expansions and renovations.

THE FIRST SCHOOL BUS

The neighborhood school concept is not new. The early schools were built within walking distance of clusters of homes. Despite this, there was still need for students to walk a distance, since the houses were usually many hundreds, if not thousands, of feet apart.

It was not until the one-room schools began to consolidate that there was need for a faster way for students to get to school than walking. Most residents had horses, but taking them to school was not feasible for three reasons. First, the schools were hardly big enough for both students and horses, since the ratio of horses to people was about 5:1. Secondly, the horses were needed on the farms and could not be assigned a student(s) for an entire day. Finally, feeding, caring for and cleaning up after the horses would require additional space and/or personnel. To solve the transportation problem, schools paid

A typical early school bus before motorized buses were used.

farmers a trifle amount to transport students from distant places to the consolidated schools.

The first means of conveyance were "kid wagons." This translated into any kind of wagon on which students would ride. Later "kid wagons" would be wagons converted for this purpose and would have benches on which to sit. Earlier ones were not covered, so students had to take blankets with them to protect them from the cold weather. Later ones were covered, but only with a roof and leather sides. The front was not covered and cold winds still chilled the riders.

The first motorized buses in Wadsworth started to appear about 1927, when farmers built a wooden box on a truck chassis and placed wooden benches inside for seats. In the summer, when school was no longer in session, the boxes were taken off the truck chassis, and the farmer would use his truck in the normal way. Only Wadsworth Township Centralized School was served with bus transportation; the Wadsworth City Schools district was not. Students still needed to walk to school if they resided within the city limits.

THE WADSWORTH ACADEMY

As population grew, so did the need for more and varied subject matter for students who were not challenged academically. In 1830, the first log Congregational church was being finished, and some of the village elders saw an opportunity to utilize the church building during the week, when religious services were not being conducted. Frederick Brown, George Lyman, Dr. George Pardee, William Eyles and Horatio Warner suggested that they use the church for an academy. The members of the church agreed that it would be good for the village and offered the space without cost, except that students would need to provide their own desks and chairs.

The committee cited above employed a student from Western Reserve College (then in Hudson but now in Cleveland), George W. Barnes, to be the first teacher. Loren Kennedy and Isaac Van Tassel followed him when he resigned and stayed until 1834, when the soon-to-be-famous John McGregor would become the teacher.

McGregor had come to Sharon Center to teach in an academy before arriving in Wadsworth. He was originally from Hamilton, Scotland, but escaped to Vermont when his ill-fated attempt to overthrow the monarchy failed. Whatever his political views, they did not interfere with his becoming one of the greatest teachers that Wadsworth has known. He instituted a

The Octagon, situated north of where the present First Christian Church is locatec and also used for Wadsworth Academy.

curriculum that included grammar, logic, philosophy, chemistry, surveying, algebra and Latin—a curriculum almost unheard of in this part cf the country in that era. So great was his impact on students that they placed a marker on his grave almost forty years after he died. McGregor left Wadsworth to found the *Stark County Democrat* but wanted to be buried in the "old ground" of Woodlawn Cemetery in Wadsworth.

McGregor's reputation as a scholar was known widely in education circles and was cited in books on curriculum. His expansion on traditional curriculum was almost revolutionary. Some of the more advanced students were introduced not only to Latin, but to Greek as well. What started out in Wadsworth education as a bleak smattering of basic subjects developed into an advanced course of study that prepared local students for the wider world. Wadsworth, indeed, went from bleak to Greek.

HIGHER EDUCATION

One of the outcomes of education is that one learns how much he or she does not know. When the early settlers of Wadsworth had no education, they were thirsty for at least some knowledge. After they received a little, they wanted more. It follows, then, that after the students went to the Wadsworth Academy under the tutelage of John McGregor, they had a need for more depth in the areas of logic, philosophy, mathematics and history. To this end, the learned people of Wadsworth sought out institutions that would broaden their children's educational horizons. Western Reserve College in Hudson was that institution.

Eugene Pardee, son of Judge Allen Pardee, and Edward Brown, son of Judge Frederick Brown, attended Western Reserve College in Hudson, Ohio, where the early settlers had founded the "Yale of the West" in 1826. Western Reserve College was moved from Hudson to Cleveland in 1882 to become Western Reserve University and, later still, Case-Western Reserve University.

THE MENNONITE COLLEGE

Wadsworth was chosen to be the site of the Mennonite College because it had a railroad, was centrally located among the Mennonite communities in Pennsylvania, Michigan and Indiana and the countryside was beautiful and rural.

Reverend Ephriam Hunsberger purchased a 103-acre farm west of the Center for $6,695, kept twenty-four acres for the college and sold the rest. In essence, he got the land for free.

It took three years for the General Mennonite Conference to raise enough money to build the thirty-four- by fifty-four-foot, three-story red brick building. Reverend Hunsberger served as the driving force, combining the efforts of the Wadsworth community with those of the Mennonite communities cited earlier and the General Conference.

After the college was finished, it was determined that the kitchen would be in the basement, the next two floors would be used for classrooms and the third floor for dormitories. The first occupants were not Mennonites. Reverend James Encel, a Disciple minister, rented rooms in the nearly finished building in 1865. His tenure was short-lived and somewhat demeaned by stories about his fairly large student body engaging in fun activities rather than studying.

The college cost $12,245 to build and was dedicated on October 13 and 14 in a ceremony that was coupled with the meeting of the General Conference. The first classes began on January 2, 1868, with twenty-four men, of whom only thirteen were from Mennonite families. Tuition was set at $100 annually, but students had to volunteer three hours a day to maintain the building and services. The $100 included instruction, lodging, washing, fuel and light. Admission was contingent upon the student being of good character and being between eighteen and thirty years of age.

Christian Showalter of Iowa was the first principal. The entire course of study covered three years and included courses to prepare men for the ministry and/or missionary work. Carl Justus van der Smissen, from Friedrichstadt, Germany, came to teach philosophy, but his stern and demanding European-trained professional demeanor was not a good fit for the more relaxed American midwestern students. As a result, there was much dissention within the faculty and between him and his students.

The Mennonite College, where Isham School is today.

Debt began to mount. Money needed to help Mennonite immigrants escape persecution in Europe was draining the treasury, and enrollment was waning. These two factors caused the General Conference to transform the school from male-only to coeducational; to become a normal school rather than a religious school; and to accept all denominations. Only the German and theology departments would continue as ordained by the original charter.

The normal school, with former Union School superintendent A.B. Stuzman as head, increased in enrollment, while enrollment for German and philosophy dropped dramatically. Brothers A.B. Shelly and Daniel Shelly followed Stuzman and increased the enrollment to sixty. L.S. Schimmel joined the brothers and together opened the Excelsior Normal School to prepare students to become teachers in the public schools. This strategy was so successful for the Excelsior School that it overshadowed what had been the original mission of the school. As a result, the General Conference discontinued the Mennonite College in 1878 and sold the building. The only vestige of the college is memorialized in the name of the road on which it was built: College Street.

THE DAGUE COLLEGIATE INSTITUTE

M.D. Dague of Doylestown purchased the unused Mennonite College to move his son's Collegiate Institute from Chillicothe to Wadsworth in 1876. Thomas Jefferson Dague, the son, thought that the institute would either supplement the Union School or replace it. Neither was the right call since the $200 in tuition was an extravagance, given that his school did not offer any more than the tuition-free Union School did.

Thomas attended the North School (the second school built in Wadsworth) and then moved to Western Star and went to that school. He served in the Civil War and, upon being discharged, opened a private academy in Doylestown. He then decided to go to Miami University to pursue an education and received bachelor's and master's degrees. It was after receiving his degrees that he went to Chillicothe and then later to Wadsworth.

There is no record of how long Dague operated the school, but in view of the fact that the Western Reserve Normal College moved into the building in 1885, it would appear the institute was no longer viable after that date.

The Western Reserve Normal College

The Mennonite College building and/or property seemed to be destined always to be committed to education. After the Collegiate Institute closed, Professor J.B. Eberly, who operated a normal school in Smithville, approached officials from Wadsworth and asked them to buy the vacant college building and to build a normal school adjacent to it. In return, Eberly would move his normal school from Smithville to Wadsworth. Wadsworth officials accepted the offer and floated a $25,000 bond issue to construct the school.

In 1885, Eberly moved his school as agreed and enrolled 100 students almost immediately. In 1888, the township erected the building it promised, and shortly thereafter, enrollment reached 245. Also in 1888, the school was chartered as the Western Reserve Normal College. The name Western Reserve was used often in schools, both here, in Hudson and in Cleveland. (Some historians believe that there is a connection, but this author was not able to find any conclusive direct relationship between the schools.)

With a minimal tuition rate of only twenty-four dollars a year, students could become teachers after completing the course of study. Women were permitted to live in the converted Mennonite College building, but men had to find quarters of their own, most living with local residents. Girls paid an additional seventy-four dollars per year for room and board, including a furnished room, light and heat. The room and board fee was reduced if the girl opted to eat on her own.

In 1892, brothers E.A. and F.A. Day became directors of the school that then became the Wadsworth Normal School. Instruction was presented in five departments: normal, academic, musical, commercial and elocutionary. The academic courses included Latin, Greek, German, algebra, geometry, composition and rhetoric. These courses were expansions of courses taken in high school. The "normal" courses were directed toward teacher training. The school closed in 1896, with the building being transferred to the Wadsworth Township trustees and used for storage, extra classroom space when the village schools were overcrowded and for private apartments. It ultimately became the site of Wadsworth Township Centralized School in 1915.

Burke Hinsdale

A history of higher education in Wadsworth would not be complete without relating the life of Burke Hinsdale, cousin of the Pardees, sons of two sisters

Burke Hinsdale, noted American educator who was from Wadsworth.

(Hinsdale's mother was Clarinda Eyles Hinsdale, and Aaron Pardee's mother was Evelyn Eyles Pardee).

Born on March 28, 1837, on a farm on Stony Ridge Road and east of Vacation Ridge, summer home of the Pardees, Burke Hinsdale worked on the family farm but had a strong desire to become educated. He went to schools in Wadsworth from time to time but felt he still wanted more. He enrolled in Hiram's institute but had to take time off to earn enough money to return for succeeding semesters.

While at Hiram, Hinsdale met James A. Garfield (later to become president of the United States) and considered him a mentor. Even after Garfield became president, he kept a close association with Hinsdale, regarding him to be of superior intelligence and wisdom. Garfield encouraged Hinsdale to continue his studies, encouragement Hinsdale did not really need since he detested farm labor and wanted to escape from it at almost any cost. Money was in short supply, but Hinsdale was fortunate enough to be selected as a tutor at the Eclectic Institute at Hiram, an appointment awarded him by the principal, James A. Garfield.

In 1869, Hinsdale became professor of philosophy, English literature and political science at Hiram College. The next year, at age thirty-three, he was chosen as president of Hiram College, Garfield's successor. The institute had become Hiram College in 1867.

Hinsdale's scholarly bent resulted in writing three books about theological subjects. In 1880, the Republican National Committee commissioned him to write a campaign biography of Garfield. Garfield was assassinated in 1881, whereupon Hinsdale wrote a memorial for the fallen president, *President Garfield and Education.* At Mrs. Garfield's request, he edited two volumes of *The Works of James Abram Garfield.*

Hinsdale continued to be president of Hiram but then was called to become superintendent of the Cleveland Public Schools in 1884, during which time he wrote *The Old Northwest.* From Cleveland, he was invited to the University of Michigan to teach science and art. He was revered at Michigan and is still remembered for his distinguished service for writing *The History of the University of Michigan* and other books as well.

Remarkably, Hinsdale was able to become one of America's great names in education without ever having received even a bachelor's degree and had only sporadic high school instruction. Despite these "weaknesses," he received honorary degrees from Williams College, Bethany College, the Ohio State University, Hiram College and Ohio University.

Part V

The Press

The *Wadsworth Enterprise*: All the News that Fits...to Print

Newspapers did not exist in Wadsworth prior to 1866, when John L. Clark, Wadsworth's first newspaper editor, started the small but newsy newspaper for Wadsworth residents, the *Wadsworth Enterprise*.

The motto of the *New York Times* is "All the News That's Fit to Print." The motto of the *Enterprise* could well have been "All the News That Fits to Print" since the paper was so small that it could *fit* only select stories in the small page utilized by the paper.

What was considered newsworthy then would probably not be newsworthy now, but it satisfied the perceived needs of the day, minimal though they were. News about how to control potato bugs garnered more prominence than news of greater importance.

The paper's tenuous beginning started when the Medina County Farmer's Insurance Company became dissatisfied with printing services being rendered by the *Akron Beacon*. It decided to print in house; however, none in the company knew anything about printing and did not want to add printing to the insurance business. They retained George A. Root from Sharon to purchase a printing press in Cincinnati, pay for it in installments and assume all the printing needs for the insurance company. The company would pay Root for his services, affording him enough to pay for the press. Wallace Root, George's brother, was a printer for the *Beacon* but quit his job there and came to Wadsworth to operate the press—a hand one at that.

After the brothers paid off the press from money they received from the insurance company, they began the *Enterprise*, with John Clark becoming a writer and part owner. Later, he became the sole owner of the paper, as

Left: John Clark, editor of the *Enterprise*.

Below: The building in which the *Enterprise* was printed.

well as the first superintendent of the village schools. This was particularly noteworthy since he had a limited education, but his practice in writing, as well as the business skills he learned as a printer, propelled him to higher lofts.

In 1891, Clark sold the paper to Orin C. Baker, who began publishing it as the *Wadsworth Banner and Enterprise.* The *Banner*, owned by James E. Corry and sold to Baker, had been in publication since 1885 and was in competition with the *Enterprise.* A short time later, the paper became the *Banner-Press.*

Other local-only papers that originated in Wadsworth but did not last for any period of time were the *Wadsworth Advance*, the *Wadsworth Register* and the *Wadsworth News* (not related to the later paper by the same name).

The *Young Folks Gem*: All that Litters Brings in Gold

George C. Bennett's name is legendary in Wadsworth history, but it is almost forgotten. Some historians and local dignitaries of the time are reputed to have forgotten his name on purpose because they thought George was a lowlife. He was a gangly teenager and strange-looking boy who was jeered at by other boys and laughed at by girls. He did not fit in and became reclusive. He resented the manner in which he was treated and rebelled by becoming a social outcast.

He had few talents and was unable to develop those he had because of his status as a rejected boy. To make money, he would do odd jobs wherever he could. One such job was to hoe corn for a local farmer. Then, as now, the plantain leaf was a never-ending nemesis to farmers. George had the cure, however, and spent the first three dollars he made hoeing the plantain leaf to pay for the following advertisement in a newspaper: "Ho, farmers! Send twenty-five cents for a cheap, sure way to rid your fields of the plantain leaf evil!" When the quarters began coming at a surprising rate, he was ecstatic. Without delay, he sent back the "cure" for the plantain leaf scourge: "Pull up the weeds and burn them…The only cure known."

Farmers complained bitterly to town officials, but there were no laws prohibiting this since the "cure" would certainly work. The farmers lost their quarters, but George had amassed more than enough to build a small structure at Clark Corners on his father's land for a paper that allegedly contained obscene literature, lists of pornographic books and commentary on some of the books.

When George Bennett's *Young Folks Gem* outgrew its space in previous locations, it was printed at the *Enterprise*. Even the *Enterprise* had to purchase more equipment to print the nearly half million copies.

Bennett soon outgrew his small "yaller shack," as it was called, and moved to a larger structure in Sharon as orders for his paper increased dramatically. He was arrested for sending obscene materials through the mail, but his father bailed him out for $500 and the boy was free to function as before. This time he offered premiums to people who would sell subscriptions of his "gem" throughout the country. His offer of a six-shooter brought many takers, but the real "take" was a toy gun with six corks on a string. In many cases, the takers did not get even that in return for their offer to solicit subscriptions.

Not all of Wadsworth's residents were scandalized by his "unsavory" character. Unsavory as it might have been, it did not detract from his ability to enlarge a tabloid from rural Wadsworth to an almost worldwide circulation, boasting 450,000 copies in 1875. His own former teacher, Peter Cherry, accepted a position with his not-so-lustrous student to write articles for the *Young Folks Gem*. The *Enterprise* was retained to print the ever-expanding number of copies needed. The post office was raised to a fourth-grade rating and the postmaster's salary was increased because of the growing volume he handled.

According to an interview with Peter Cherry in the June 19, 1932 edition of the *Akron Beacon Journal*, George Bennett was, indeed, a social reject who vented his pent-up anger on those who taunted him by doing whatever necessary to become someone important. Cherry did not allude to any of the "unsavory" characteristics cited above about obscene or pornographic literature, but he did admit to his less-than-honest premiums offer for services rendered. The Wadsworth Area Historical Society is in possession of one such premium, donated from the Stauffer collection, of a picture of an innocent child—which assuredly would not be considered pornographic—mounted in a frame measuring approximately twenty-eight by twenty-four inches.

One of the persons who did not prosper from his success was Bennett himself. Without a strong base of direction to lead a clean life, he fell victim to the ways of the newly rich and died at the age of almost twenty-three. At least one account of his age puts him at twenty-one when he died. He was buried at the Norton Cemetery on Medina Line Road and was laid to rest by his employees. Not even death seemed to end his life: townsfolk swear that his ghost walked around Wadsworth for years.

Part VI

The 1900s: Motoring into the Future

Andy Auble

Although the automobile had been invented a few years earlier, it had not made its appearance in Wadsworth until after the turn of the century.

Credit is given to Andy Auble for bringing the automobile to light by opening the first repair garage in the country. This historic site was located on the north side of College Street about two hundred feet west of the square. The pump was on the street and his "repair garage" farther back. According to the *Akron Motorist*, Auble's garage and gasoline pump were the first in the country. Whether this is accurate is in question; however, several historians have thrown down the gauntlet to the rest of the nation to see if anyone would contest the claim. To date, none has. With the gasoline pump being part of his repair garage, Andy also gets credit for having the first filling station in the United States.

Andy Auble started out with a bicycle shop but realized that the automobile would soon overtake transportation and decided to be proactive. He went to Cleveland in 1901 and drove the one-cylinder Oldsmobile to Wadsworth, where everyone turned out to see it. It was only the fifty-sixth vehicle that R.E. Olds manufactured and cost $600.

Andy was known throughout Wadsworth as a spirited person who was not afraid to lead toward the future, despite not knowing what the future held. He rode his bicycle from Wadsworth to Chicago to the World's Fair, a distance of close to four hundred miles, given the route he took.

Before Andy left Wadsworth for Akron to open the first garage there, he tried to sell cars in Wadsworth. Richard F. Weaver purchased the first car, and then Andy went to Akron and sold the first automobile in Akron. For Andy, the move to Akron was almost as historic as starting the first garage

An early filling station. Wadsworth had the first "filling" station in the United States.

An early car, but probably not Andy Auble's, the automobile pioneer in Wadsworth.

and filling station in Wadsworth. He sold thirty-five Oldsmobiles in just three weeks.

The Auble family was prominent in both building and governing Wadsworth in earlier times and has descendants still living here who continue that legacy.

THE FIRST STREETCAR: THE SUGAR BILL

In the Connecticut Western Reserve, the distance between the center of a township to the center of the adjoining ones was five miles—a good distance when only rudimentary transportation was available. Transportation was difficult, even with more "improved" roads—improved only in that some of the dirt surfaces had hardened from constant usage. The streetcar served to give people a bit more mobility in that cars were almost nonexistent.

Since the railroad had come through several years earlier, the Northern Ohio Traction and Light Company, the streetcar line developers, decided to parallel the existing tracks to take advantage of the already-leveled grading barriers that would have made streetcar navigation impossible. Despite this, the roadbed had to be graded even further because the electric streetcar did not have the power to climb the steep inclines as did engines. Massive steam-powered shovels were brought in to level the untamed barriers.

Work to construct the seven-mile line from Barberton to Wadsworth began in 1906, using more than ten tons of copper wire, hundreds of cedar poles to carry the wires and thousands of ties placed on a bed of coarse aggregate to carry the streetcar. In addition to challenging grading problems, the streetcar track had to cross over the Erie Railroad tracks at Rockcut—a large rock formation—in Sherman.

Four stops were made from Barberton to the Wadsworth terminus: Sherman, Western Star, Silver Creek and, finally, Wadsworth. The streetcar entered Broad Street from East Street and went west on Broad Street, through the square and onto College Street, where it stopped and backed into the north park to take on eastbound passengers for the run back to Barberton. The car ended at the "loop" in Barberton, from which riders could change cars to go to Akron. Most of the people worked in Barberton and did not need the extra service to Akron; however, on special occasions, people from Wadsworth went to Akron to shop and would use the entire line for transportation.

On April 8, 1907, Dr. Robert Johnson, then mayor of Wadsworth, greeted the fifteen hundred witnesses to the arrival of the first streetcar and then

An early streetcar.

drove the last gilded spike into the ground at the confluence of the East Park and High Street using a gilded sledge. At four o'clock that afternoon, the streetcar made its maiden journey into Barberton with Joe Bender—actor, restaurateur, real estate owner and philanthropist—as the ticket taker.

Electricity for the streetcar was produced by a huge generator located in Barberton. Two long arms projected from the car to make contact with the two wires above, therein carrying electricity to the motor on the car. Not infrequently, the arms would become separated from the wires and the car would stop, having lost its source of electricity. In these cases, the motorman would take a long pole and realign the arms to the wires above. When this happened at night, he would have to go outside in total darkness, since the loss of electricity also meant loss of lights. In cold weather, realigning the arms was especially difficult, and it was not uncommon for the car to be delayed several minutes, making schedules erratic.

There are many stories about streetcar happenings. One of the oddest involves a young lad who went to Barberton to buy five pounds of sugar. On the way home, the bag ripped open, and rather than let it go to waste, he began eating it. Those sitting nearby were taken by his plight and decided to help him with his frugality by eating some of it with him. By the time he got home, all the sugar was gone. His mother was furious and began berating him for not returning with the sugar. While taking the wrath she was handing out, he told her exactly what had happened, thinking she would be mollified with his explanation. She wasn't. In fact, she did not believe him. Later, she learned that he was being truthful. From that time on, the family, the neighbors and the riders on the streetcar began calling him "Sugar Bill," a name that followed him throughout his life. Common among locals was the tale that the car on which he ate the sugar was from then on called the Sugar Bill. It is believed the motorman, who lived near Sugar Bill, unofficially dubbed the car that name.

Other stories were told about people who had little or nothing else to do, so they would board the car in Wadsworth, pay the tiny fare to go to Barberton and return without getting off there, thus not paying for a return trip. Their motivation was to merely go for a ride or to chat with people on the car.

Sherman, one of the stops, had a bar that many Wadsworth residents frequented on Saturday nights. Although the bar stayed open until midnight, it would be almost devoid of patrons after eleven o'clock because the last car to Wadsworth came then. The motorman's son, who now lives in New York and who is in his mid-eighties at this writing, remembers his father's complaining about that run since most of the riders were inebriated and would cause problems on the car or get sick from the trolley swaying left and right.

With the general population preferring the automobile and the emergence of public buses for transportation, the streetcar made its last run on December 31, 1934. For twenty-seven years, however, it expanded Wadsworth's travel horizons by at least seven miles and sometimes fourteen.

The First Telephone: Number Please

While we believe the telephone to be a recent invention, a telephone line ran through Wadsworth in 1880, connecting Akron to Medina. This did not imply that people in Wadsworth had telephones; there was only one in the village in 1880—at Brouse's harness shop. It was not until fifteen years later, in 1895, that a small group of Wadsworth businessmen organized the Home Telephone Company (later, the Wadsworth General Electric Company) with $10,000, a huge sum for the times.

Reverend F.G. McCauley, Richard F. Weaver, Oliver L. Nolf, William Oplinger, Charles L. Wertz and Milton and Jacob Leatherman began their venture in a building on the southwest corner of the square, somewhat back from Main and College Streets. The "operators" were all women (a practice that still exists largely today) and had to be trained to "operate" the cumbersome lines and plugs that were part of the telephone mechanism in the early days.

By 1895, Wadsworth had about 120 telephone subscribers. Operators would ask the subscriber for the number being called (in the early days, names rather than numbers were used). They would then use a long stick to engage the connection or to remove it. There was no outside electricity to energize the ringing device to the operator; the subscriber would turn a crank attached to a generator to alert the operator.

When the system outgrew the small building housing the operators, the telephone equipment was moved to the second floor of a building closer to College Street, approximately one hundred feet west of Main Street. The operating system was essentially the same used in the previous building and served about four hundred subscribers.

The popularity of the telephone to talk over wide distances was intriguing to Wadsworth residents, since, as was mentioned in previous accounts, houses were far apart, especially in the township. The telephone compressed the distance and saved time and energy in communicating. Nonetheless, not every household had a telephone.

In 1905, the Star Telephone Company of Ashland, Ohio, purchased the Wadsworth General Electric Company. This new company brought vast improvements for the time and increased subscribership considerably. It rapidly outgrew the small quarters on College Street and moved to a room on the second floor of a building on the newly built Myers block. The technical improvements were primitive compared to modern-day technology but revolutionary in 1905.

Shortly after the Star Telephone Company began, so many subscribers were added that it outgrew its recently occupied quarters in the Myers block and moved to the east side of High Street in 1921. There were three local boards and three long-distance boards operated by at least three women. At the beginning, phone service was available only from 6:00 a.m. until 10:00 p.m. Later, the hours were expanded, and by 1921, service was generally available all day and all night.

Telephone rates were about two dollars a month and were billed on a penny postcard and written by hand. By today's standards, long-distance calls were expensive and somewhat difficult to access. In a call to Cleveland, the Wadsworth operator would call an Akron operator, the Akron operator would call a Cleveland operator, the Cleveland operator would ask the caller for the Cleveland number requested and then she would connect the two parties. Those who did not want to pay for a call if the person on the other end were not available would call person to person. If the person were

Typical operators with the early telephone system in Wadsworth.

not available, the caller paid nothing. The less expensive call would be the station-to-station one in which the caller paid the toll fee regardless of who answered. Small communities that maintained independently owned local systems presented more serious problems because calling from one small system to another required additional steps. It was not unheard of to wait for several minutes before completing a call between Wadsworth and Rittman, a distance of five miles.

In an age when people long for a human voice to greet them instead of an automated voice system, Wadsworth's early telephone operators not only asked for the number in person, but were repositories of local knowledge. Some operators would recognize the voice of the caller trying to reach another person, and tell that person that the person being called was not home but would return later.

The police did not have radios in their cars, so the operators would signal them when they received a call for an emergency by pressing a button on their boards that activated a blue light on the square. When the patrolman saw the light—sometimes many minutes later—he would go to the telephone booth in the square and call the operator. She would relay the information about the emergency and the patrolman would make his emergency run to the victim, providing the victim was still there, alive or still needed assistance.

Until the middle of the twentieth century, most of the telephones in Wadsworth were on a party line. Fortunate people had only two or three on a line, but township people had as many as twelve. Each phone had a different ring, and only the people in the household for which that ring was intended were supposed to answer the phone. Needless to say, this restriction was not always observed, much to the consternation of people who would hear their private conversations on the lips of others in the community later on. People would devise code words for events that only the two people talking would understand. This worked until the callers would slip and say the actual word, therein giving away the code.

Jay G. Welday, a legend in Wadsworth with the phone companies from 1909 until his retirement in 1950, did everything from climbing poles, stringing wires, installing telephones or whatever else needed to be done mechanically or administratively during his tenure. His daughter, Dorothy Welday, still lives in Wadsworth at this writing.

CITY GOVERNMENT AND A NEW TOWN HALL

With the increase in population in Wadsworth from 227 in 1818 to about 1,700 in 1860, local government had to become more sophisticated and formalized to grow with the needs of the population. For years, a few townspeople would make unilateral decisions and move forward with the results of the decisions without public approbation. There did not seem to be much change in the cast of characters after 1860, but the decision-making process began to conform to then legal standards.

Aaron Pardee, his son, Henry Pardee, and Dr. C.N. Lyman drew up the papers of incorporation before 1866, but the village was not incorporated officially until then. The first election was held in the Traver Carriage Works office on High Street (across from the Traver-Johnson House, the Wadsworth Area Historical Society headquarters), with the election board composed of Luman Mills, H.J. Traver and John Lugenbeel as judges, and John Houston and an unidentified citizen as clerks. As of this writing, no records have been found of that meeting. From the scanty newspaper accounts of the time, there seemed to be little interest in the election—not unsurprisingly, since formalized governance was an unknown to most residents.

Following the first election, a general election followed to select village officials. Aaron Pardee was elected mayor; John C. Houston, recorder; and Dr. C.N. Lyman, William F. Boyer, John Lytle, Dr. W.T. Ridenour and Luman P. Mills, trustees. John J. Woodward was appointed treasurer on April 24, 1866. On July 25, Houston resigned as recorder and John Clark succeeded him. Aaron Pardee was appointed as the first attorney for the village in addition to being mayor.

To house the new government, the village needed a bigger and more commodious structure than the temporary ones used in years past. Previously, village business was transacted in homes or anywhere else people met. One year after the first election took place, plans for a new town hall were conceived and executed. For a cost of $5,000, the brick structure was erected that included a place for government, a room for holding vagrants or other miscreants, a post office, council room and a meeting room with a stage that had entrance and exit doors and a drop curtain.

One of the early meeting places for town government.

Despite the town hall being identified as such, it well could have been promoted as the local theatre. There were more activities involving plays, skits, speeches and performances than almost anything else, probably because it was the only "theatre" in the village. Captain Theodore Wolbach, of photography fame, starred in the first play given in the theatre part of the town hall, *The Ticket-of-Leave Man*, by Tom Taylor, the popular nineteenth-century English dramatist. The story, about a person who had a ticket-of-leave (paperwork given to released prisoners), was considered a coincidence since the town hall had a jail of sorts within it. There are personal memories of people talking about this as late as the mid-twentieth century, albeit probably less often and less dramatically than in earlier times. The significance of this statement is that the village had been so devoid of cultural events of this magnitude that the experience remained imprinted indelibly on the minds of people for years.

THE OPERA HOUSE, JOE BENDER AND THE FIRST PICTURE SHOW

Although the town hall included an auditorium and a stage, it was not long before community interest in the arts outgrew the small accommodation it provided.

Dr. J.F. Detweiler, whose house was on the southwest corner of Broad and South Lyman Streets, built the Opera House behind his house in 1891. The immediate motivation for building it was to stage the Coleman and Heagler Big City Minstrels, produced by two Wadsworth locals whose production was a smashing success at the Opera House but failed when it went on the road.

Just thirty-nine workdays after groundbreaking, the building was ready for the Minstrels. The seven hundred seats were filled the whole time that the show ran. People who could afford to do so could sit in one of the two box seats near the thirty-seven- by fifty-foot stage and await the huge curtain opening for the performances.

The building was lighted with gaslights at the beginning but converted to electricity when it became more popular and readily available. The gaslights needed a compressor to keep them going in such a large building. At best, they were only minimally effective, and when the pressure ebbed, the show would have to stop until more pressure could be built up.

In addition to the Minstrels, other shows were brought in from "the road." Notable ones included *Fast Mail*, *The Tornado*, *The Royal Slave*, *Si Perkins* and *My Wife's Family*.

In 1913, at age thirty-three, Joe Bender, a rags-to-riches legacy in Wadsworth, purchased the Opera House from Dr. Detweiler and made many needed improvements. He installed a new roof, excavated a tunnel from the stage to the office, changed the seating to create a center aisle, built a new lobby, lighted the walkway from Broad Street to the Opera House, piped water into the building, installed a fire hose connection, added two projectors to the movie projection booth and made a variety of other minor improvements.

Joe acted in many of the performances, particularly in Shakespearean plays, with a voice that filled the auditorium. He also wrote plays and continued to bring in the creative works of others. The Opera House was indeed *the* place for entertainment in Wadsworth, especially after it became the first movie theatre in Wadsworth in 1914. Movies were shown only on Saturdays at first but later every evening.

After Joe's pioneering movie theatre entertainment in Wadsworth (called picture shows then), others saw how popular they were and sought to become involved as well. About 1920, William Standen opened the Strand Theatre on Broad Street. In 1922, John Damm bought the theatre. Damm wanted to have a monopoly on movie theatres and approached Joe to purchase the Opera House. Damm was in partnership with Norman Stein (later mayor

The Opera House, Wadsworth's recreation emporium.

of Wadsworth), Sam Burgess and C.C. Patterson—all doing business as the Wadsworth Amusement Company. They purchased the Opera House on January 1, 1923, for $11,000. One of their first moves was to close the Opera House and end its nearly forty-year legacy.

The Opera House was demolished in 1935, silencing echoes of lines spoken by famous and not-so-famous actors, extinguishing the flicker of gaslights in the now dark house and calming the whirr of a primitive movie projector struggling to cast its image on the bedsheet screen. But most of all, its demise buried the only memory of William Jennings Bryan speaking his eloquent heart to Wadsworth for the last time.

Joe Bender (1880–1967) is a piece of nineteenth-century Wadsworth history but a contemporary as well, since hundreds of people still remember the unaffected, generous, penurious, talented, philanthropic, industrious, humble man who started out in life shooing flies from horses in a blacksmith shop near the house in which he was born. His pay was only a few cents per week, but it was the beginning of a lifestyle that would make him a wealthy man in later life. After the fly-shooing occupation, he worked at the Match, the most common way to identify the Ohio Match Company, for five cents per hour until he became a foreman over the first four match machines, making twenty cents per hour. He bought a popcorn stand and sold the snack on the street corner in the Center, took some classes in business, started the *Plain Dealer* and *Leader* newsstand (where he also sold sandwiches) and opened a restaurant, at which he served tables and his wife, Kate, did much of the cooking.

He started a billboard and poster advertising business but sold it to the General Outdoor Advertising Company. His bent, however, was always with the stage, and he felt that it was important to encourage people, especially young people, to nurture their creativity and to serve their communities. He was an example of what he preached. Until his death, he wrote poems, gave Shakespearean readings and quietly donated land and real estate to the churches and to the community. Notable of these two recipients were Sacred Heart Church—to which he gave land for the school, office buildings and other brick-and-mortar projects—and the City of Wadsworth, to which he gave extensively in the development of Durling Park. He gave land to the city for the road that used to go through Durling Park and the south end of East Street for a bridge over the railroad tracks.

Part VII

Early Medical Professionals: Corn Plasters and Country Doctors

The Physicians

It must be noted that, before beginning a history of early medical people and early medicine, the reader must remember that medicine was primitive in the early settlement days when comparing it to what we have grown to expect today.

As was stated in previous sections, Dr. C.N. Lyman was the only physician in the village during the earliest days of the settlement. Most of his life is chronicled in those sections and will not be repeated here.

Dr. Nathan Everhard, born in 1841 on the other side of the south line of Wadsworth Township, began practicing medicine in Wadsworth in 1867 in his home at 180 Main Street, where the Wadsworth Towers are presently located. He was the first of the Pennsylvania Dutch pioneers who became a physician from the area. One of eleven children of John and Mary Harter Everhard, he grew up farming, as did others of the Pennsylvania Dutch community. His brother was also a physician but practiced elsewhere.

Dr. Everhard married Ella M. Finley Everhard, after whom the Wadsworth Public Library is named. She donated the Leiter House to the city in the early 1920s so that the tiny collection of books serving as a library could be located in a more commodious setting. The house served this function for many years and was replaced by a new library in 1950. This library, then, was replaced again with the present library in 2003.

In addition to practicing medicine in Wadsworth, Dr. Everhard was also the surgeon for the Western Division of the Erie Railroad and a member of the board of censors of the Medical Department of Wooster University, then located in Cleveland, where he held an endowed chair. Wooster University later merged with the Western Reserve Medical College.

Dr. F.F. Falk, one of Wadsworth's early doctors.

On the village scene, Dr. Everhard was very instrumental in helping to develop the Ohio Companies and in building the present structure of Grace Lutheran Church.

Dr. Wallace A. Briggs, almost a local (born in Sharon Township), married Ella Pardee, the third daughter of Aaron Pardee. After graduating from the University of Michigan Medical Department and doing postgraduate work in New York, Berlin and Paris, he moved to California, where he later died. While still active in medicine, he achieved the prestigious honor of becoming the dean of medical professionals in California. Although he did not practice in Wadsworth, he was highly regarded as a native son who reaped high honors in the field of medicine.

Dr. George H. Wuchter was in the first class that graduated from Wadsworth High School in 1877 and the first graduate of the school to become a physician. He studied with the venerated Dr. Lyman and then went to the University of Pennsylvania Medical College, from which he graduated in 1880.

Although River Styx was a swampy piece of land in the late 1880s, Dr. Wuchter began his practice there before coming to Wadsworth. During the Spanish-American War, he became the only surgeon with the Eighth Ohio and Thirty-third Michigan Infantries. During his stint in these divisions, he had a white horse that carried him to the wounded soldiers on the battlefield. Following the war and his return to Wadsworth, he kept the horse and was identified by it.

During the Cuban campaign, he contracted health problems that caused him to quit his practice of medicine. Instead, he became an undertaker with his father's firm until the latter's death and then joined W.H. Oplinger in preparing bodies for burial.

Concerning Dr. Wilbert Hinsdale, the Hinsdale name appears often in Wadsworth history. Burke Hinsdale was president of Hiram College, among other achievements, and his brother, Wilbert B., became a physician who practiced in Wadsworth until he was invited to join the staff at the University of Michigan as a professor of internal and clinical medicine, dean of the college and medical director of the University of Michigan Hospital.

As was his brother, Wilbert was born in Wadsworth Township on Stony Ridge Road and worked on the family farm. Their parents' fondest wish was that their children would become educated adults, a dream that was realized with one son becoming a college president; another a dean at a prestigious medical school; a third son, a leader in scientific farming and a state representative; and a daughter, a teacher. While practicing in Wadsworth, Dr. Hinsdale had an office in the Odd Fellows Building.

Although Dr. Frederick F. Falk's career as a physician was extremely short, he left a legacy to carry on his name in the form of his son, Fred F. Falk II, who became mayor of Wadsworth. Dr. Falk started a long line of descendants who are still active in Wadsworth circles. Robert Shaffer, his great-grandson, who at this writing is seventy-eight years old, lives on a lot that was portioned from the Fred Falk farm, a distinguished piece of land that served not only as a farm in the pioneer days of the village, but also as a landing strip for early airplanes after the Wright brothers flew theirs. The farm is also the site of Wadsworth Middle School and Wadsworth High School.

Dr. Falk's demise was attributed to his having been wounded in the Civil War a few years before his death in 1867, at age twenty-eight, leaving his widow and the future mayor, Fred II.

Dr. George A. Babbitt was born in Vermont in 1852 and attended medical lectures at Dartmouth College and Long Island College Hospital in

Brooklyn. After being certified as a physician, he traveled west but then came to Western Star at the corner of Medina Line Road and Broad Street. His residence was on the south side of the road and still stands as a monument to a physician who gained notability with his personal care to residents, especially farmers.

The writer was acquainted with several families—all now deceased—who were Dr. Babbitt's patients. Their accounts of his curing abilities regaled neighbors for years, especially the "miracles" that he was able to effect with serious diseases. Although proud that he had been invited to become associated with Cleveland City Hospital (later Metropolitan Hospital), his patients never found his equal in subsequent physicians.

Dr. Melville F. Miller, affectionately known as "Ole" Doc Miller, began practice in 1896 immediately after he graduated with a medical degree from Western Reserve College of Medicine in Cleveland.

Born in Guilford Township just west of Wadsworth Township, Dr. Miller attended the district school on the west side of Wadsworth and continued his education at the National Normal University in Lebanon, Ohio, and Thiel College in Pennsylvania.

In addition to being the epitome of a "country doctor" who cured the sick in their homes, where he would go in a horse-drawn buggy, he was active in the community. He is credited for going to the Match Shop officers to ask them to give their abandoned horse barn to the city for a hospital. Although not the first hospital in Wadsworth, it is regarded as the first "stable" hospital, since the other hospitals were small, underequipped and short-lived. He was a member of the first board of trustees of the hospital and continued in that role until he died in 1936.

Stories are rich in detail about how Dr. Miller would cure people with consumption—tuberculosis—in the days before antibiotics and modern medical interventions. His use of corn plasters was legendary. People in the early nineteenth century—now all deceased—related stories about how Doc Miller would come to the home of the patient, examine him or her and ask for some corn mush. He would bring it to a boil, put it in a cloth and place it on the almost bare chest of the patient. This writer was personally acquainted with several of the farmers who were given this treatment, many of whom lived into their eighties or nineties. There were also other stories connected to the treatment that might or might not be true, but the fact that they were recounted is indeed true. When Doc Miller would come back to visit the patient a day or two later, he would ask how he/she was feeling. On more than one occasion, the patient would feign recovery so as not to have a repetition of the "cure," since it was so painful.

The above accounts of physicians in Wadsworth constitute the ones who continued their practices for a fairly long period of time. The following are names of other ones who practiced in Wadsworth: Dr. William T. Ridenour, 1866–69; Dr. John Mikesell, 1867 (he had an office near the railroad); Dr. Daniel E. Cranz, 1877–96; and Dr. Thomas J. Ritter, circa 1880 (he then moved to Michigan).

Early Dentists

Early dentists were few and far between in the early log cabin days. Dentistry was not so sophisticated as it is today and people did not have the same focus on dental health as they do today.

It is believed that Mr. John W. Case of Sharon opened an office on the east side of Main Street in one of the newly built buildings about 1865. He allegedly had a good number of patients but did not stay in Wadsworth long. He moved to Iowa in 1866 and died a few days after arriving there.

Another early account of a dentist was found in the *Wadsworth Enterprise* in 1867, when Dr. M.A. Spence, a "surgeon dentist," announced that he would open a branch office in Wadsworth and come every other Friday in the hotel to see patients. Later that year, Mr. H.T. Clark came to Wadsworth as a "surgical and mechanical dentist" and practiced in the Odd Fellows block. He boasted a technique to extract teeth without pain, made false teeth, capped teeth with gold or silver and worked on children's teeth.

Mr. Stanley L. Thorpe opened an office in the Odd Fellows block in 1872 and was open every day except Friday, when he went to Seville to see patients there. Dr. Seeley also practiced in the Odd Fellows block toward the middle of the 1870s.

The first dentist about whom there is a recorded history with data to support all claims is Dr. Thomas C. Leiter, son of Reverend Samuel B. Leiter, a Reformed Church pastor. Dr. Leiter began his practice in 1881 after graduating from the Dental Department of the University of Michigan.

In addition to being a dentist, Dr. Leiter was also one of the organizers of the Wadsworth Salt Company. He married May Detweiler, sister of Dr. J.F. Detweiler, and was the owner of the residence on Broad Street, which Ella Everhard donated to the village for a library.

With the best of historical research, it is known that Dr. Ellis A. Kremer was the first native son to become a dentist and to begin a practice here. The son of the undertaker who buried Democrats, Dr. Kremer was the father of

Marguerite Kremer Straiton, a well-known figure in Wadsworth for years. His office was in the building in which his father embalmed bodies in the early days of Wadsworth's history.

In addition to practicing dentistry, Dr. Kremer was mayor of Wadsworth from 1897 to 1898 and served as the chairman of the Democratic Executive Committee of Medina County for fifteen years. Besides his many accomplishments, Dr. Kremer was reputed to have the largest private library in the village.

EARLY VETERINARIANS, HORSE DOCTORS, HORSE THIEVES AND HORSE INSURANCE

Early veterinarians in Wadsworth were kept busy. There were reputed to be as many horses in the village as there were people. This suggested that there should be someone to keep the horses healthy, particularly since they were the mainstay of power for early pioneers.

Andrew Harrington, Joseph Miller and Eli Chrisman began their practices here in 1884 after graduating from a Canadian veterinary school. Dr. W.C. Kreider began his practice in 1894 and was well known to farmers throughout the township as the dean of veterinarians.

Horses ruled the day, so much so that organizations sprang up to protect horses before they became ill and had to be treated by a veterinarian. Some of the "protection" however, was suspect; other sources, such as those discussed below, were legitimate.

The Union Perseverance Company for the Detection and Apprehension of Horse Thieves (UPCDAHT for short) was established to retrieve horses that had been stolen. This highly structured group held an organizational meeting on the first Saturday in February of each year and a yearly membership meeting, called Horse Company Day. Ladies were involved as well, serving dinners and acting as hostesses.

This organization was formed in 1850 with captains and express riders, one captain elected from each township belonging to the association, including Norton, Wadsworth, Guilford, Copley, Sharon, Montville, Granger, Northampton, Tallmadge, Stowe and Chippewa. The captains had eight express riders under their command from each of these townships. These express riders were to pursue any horse thief who had stolen a horse from a member-owner and make every effort to apprehend the culprit. If the express rider could not retrieve the horse, the member-owner would receive an equitable amount, not to exceed $200. Members would pay a nominal insurance fee for this service. Veterinarians would be called in to see if any harm had come to the member-owner's horse. Compensation was prorated.

Veterinarians were also in evidence at the racetrack that was built where the A-C field is presently located on College Street, west of Isham School, on the south side of the road. The track was organized in 1892 by Moran Neath, Mr. Oberholtzer, William Ault, Dr. J.F. Detweiler, Seth Baughman, Mr. Howard and others. There was an administrative structure that oversaw the activities of the track during racing season and made certain that the center of the track was filled with water in the winter for ice skating. The track succumbed to a heavy rain that brought torrents of water from the north down a steady incline and ceased to exist around the turn of the century.

Horses were king in the early days and veterinarians were their servants.

The Horse Barn: Wadsworth's New Hospital

From the earliest times that physicians began their practices in Wadsworth, there was always a semblance of a "hospital" available, meager though it was. Dr. Lyman had as hospital in his office. Dr. Bolich had a hospital in his living room to care for critically ill patients. Other doctors had "hospitals" as well.

A "house"-pital. Early hospitals were refitted houses.

It was not until November 22, 1921, that the Village of Wadsworth accepted a gift from the Ohio Match Company for a "real" hospital, with beds, an operating room, nurses and twenty-four-hour care.

The barn in which the Match kept its horses was no longer in use, since horses were no longer needed to any extent in the 1920s. Dr. Melville Miller, chronicled in an earlier section, was instrumental in approaching the officers of the Match to ask for their donation of the abandoned barn to the village.

After World War I, and only for a short period of time, the barn was used to house Match Shop workers who came to Wadsworth to supply the labor needs when the Match expanded dramatically. Because of this, there were beds, springs, mattresses, pillows, blankets, a kitchen with dishes and a laundry. Transforming it into a hospital was natural. Civic groups supplied about $50,000 to purchase equipment for the hospital. This amount, added to the $25,000 that had been earmarked for a hospital to honor World War I veterans, was enough to make the hospital viable.

The first officers of the hospital included the mayor, Dr. F. Walter Boyer, Dr. M.F. Miller, Harry E. Mills, William E. Artman and Mrs. Charles B. Allen. The hospital staff listed Dr. Miller as president and Drs. Biggs, Bolich, Everhard, E.J. Koontz and R.L. Johnson, former mayor of Wadsworth, as staff physicians.

The first superintendent of the hospital was Miss Flossie Overholt, a graduate of St. Luke's Hospital School of Nursing in Cleveland and a registered nurse. Following her were other registered nurses, Miss Edith Flickinger, Miss Merry Echols and Miss Anna McDonald.

Typically, there were only two nurses on duty, one during the day and one during the night. Emergencies were handled by one of the nurses, who would alert the doctor on call and wait for him to arrive. When a patient was brought to the hospital by ambulance, the nurse had to go into the basement, lift the screen door hook and let the patient in.

Nurses and kitchen workers canned fruits and vegetables donated or purchased from local farmers. At one time, there was a report that about three thousand half-gallon cans of food were in the pantry, including mushrooms, tomatoes, raspberries, apples, peaches, pears and assorted vegetables.

According to vital statistic records, the first boy born in the hospital was Robert Clapper and the first girl was Harriet Crawford—both in 1922. Prior to this, and for many years following, babies were born at home.

Hospital fees were extremely affordable for nearly everybody, probably because so much labor was donated and hospital personnel functioned on a bare minimum budget. Patients who could not afford treatment would

The horse stable donated to the city by the Match to serve as a hospital.

receive the same consideration as those who could, a policy imposed by the Match before it would consider donating the building to the village.

Patient rooms were on the main and the second floors. The kitchen, operating room and maintenance rooms were in the basement. Overhanging the front door was a room that was surrounded by windows. Oftentimes, long-term patients would spend their days on the sunlit "porch," and in times of overcrowded conditions, patients would be placed there.

There was a house—also owned by the Match—next to the hospital. This was used for housing the nurses, a necessity since there were so few on duty that they had to live close by in the event of immediate need.

In addition to the Match requiring treatment for everyone—irrespective of ability to pay—it also required the village to pave Garfield Street, the street on which the hospital was located. Recognizing that the hospital might not be able to continue if it lacked patient or community support, the building deed read that the building would have to be returned to the Match if the hospital discontinued operation. Not only did the hospital succeed, but it also grew to the extent that a new hospital had to be built to serve the ever-growing number of people moving to Wadsworth.

Part VIII

The Beginning of Industry: Lighting the World on Fire

The Wadsworth Salt Company

In previous sections, mention was made that the coal industry is responsible for the population growth of Wadsworth. While this was true during the pioneering days, the Ohio Companies deserve credit for contributing to the population growth even more.

The story of how the Wadsworth Salt Company—not to be confused with the Ohio Salt Company that came later—came into existence is one that is echoed many times over when researching discoveries. Henry D. Van Campen came to Wadsworth to drill for oil because he thought if there were coal here, oil could not be too far below. Instead, when he drilled into the ground about a quarter mile west of Main Street and a little north of State Street, his drill met a wide and thick vein of salt. He was dismayed, to say the least, but he decided to take advantage of this discovery and began pumping out the salt. Geologists were called in, and to their amazement, they found that the vein was vast and that the salt was of the highest quality.

In 1891, Jacob Detweiler, Dr. Thomas C. Leiter, Philip Yoder, Andrew Auble Sr., Peter Yoder, Charles A. Curtis, Dr. D.E. Cranz and Dr. F. Walter Boyer formed the Wadsworth Salt Company.

The salt was not easy to mine: It was 2,800 feet below the ground and 200 feet thick. The method used required artesian wells, of which twenty-five needed to be dug to supply enough water for extracting the salt. Salt taken from the wells was placed in drying tanks that were on the hill and stored by the railroad for easy shipping.

After a short while, the company was shipping more than seven hundred barrels of salt daily, requiring the skills of 125 men and women. So great

The initial structures of the Wadsworth Salt Company.

was the shipping volume that the railroad built a spur specifically for the shipping convenience.

Changing methods for bringing salt to the surface resulted in the company's failure by 1928. At that time, the Ohio Salt Company and the Morton Salt Company bought the equipment, but in October 1928, the entire saltworks burned to the ground in one of Wadsworth's most spectacular fires.

THE OHIO INJECTOR COMPANY

One of the earliest of the Ohio Companies was the Ohio Injector, although it was not known by that name in the beginning.

In 1883, Jacob Oberholtzer and Frank Kremer, the inventor of the Garfield injector (so named because James Garfield had been elected president of the United States three years earlier), started the company. An injector is a device that forces water into steam boilers, a mechanical necessity for steam boilers used in industry, ships and railroads.

The first injectors were manufactured in Oberholtzer's planing mill on Mechanic Street near the Erie Railroad tracks. Two years later, recognizing that the injector was a good product that was widely used, a group of men from Wadsworth invested money—some more than others—and moved the operation to the bottom of the hill on Main Street.

E.J. Young, a name synonymous with the Ohio Companies, was just an employee of the Garfield Injector Company when it started. After a short time, he bought interest in the company and catapulted his small investment into an empire that eventually would revolutionize the industrial base of the entire village and later the city.

From this fledgling beginning, the company grew even more after it was formed into the Ohio Injector Company with a new group of founders: Dr. J.F. Detweiler, Jacob S. Oberholtzer, John C. Kremer, William Hunsberger, E.J. Young, Charles Young, Frank Dremer and B.F. Sonnanstine. Later, Dr. N.S. Everhard, William E. Artman, Frank Furry (of Chicago) and Charles Ettinger joined the group.

Once again, the name of E.J. Young surfaces as the person who perfected the injector and became the on-the-road salesman. His target was primarily the railroad, since steam engines used more injectors than any other piece of equipment. Approaching railroads was often difficult, since offices were distant from small towns. By coincidence, Young met a former Wadsworthite, Charles Ettinger, who had good contacts with railroad people. Young saw that bringing Ettinger into the fold was a good move and invited him to become associated. Since Ettinger was no longer in Wadsworth, it became

The Ohio Injector in the early days of its existence.

necessary to form an Ohio Injector Company outlet in Illinois for Ettinger's convenience. Frank Furry, Ettinger's nephew, would assume administrative duties for the Chicago outlet. The move was successful, so much so that the Wadsworth Ohio Injector Company had to expand.

Wadsworth is replete with "firsts," the valve manufacturing plant being the first one in the United States. This distinction lasted until other plants emerged, recognizing the potential market for valve manufacturing as being extremely profitable.

The early Young family—E.J., Wayne (E.J.'s son), Ervin, Don and Charles—began their lives in Wadsworth without fanfare, but all received deserved praise for their contributions in building four huge plants that were the economic backbone of Wadsworth for years.

The Ohio Match Company: Its Birth and Death Made Wadsworth a "Matchless" City

The Ohio Match Company, touted to be the largest single match manufacturing plant in the world, literally set the world on fire.

Over a fifty-year period, the Match supported the lives of thousands of residents—young and old, men and women, highly technical and unskilled. Wages were low but work was steady. Even during the Great Depression, the Match continued to work—never enriching its laborers, but keeping them in simple necessities nonetheless.

Match manufacturing did not start in Wadsworth with the Ohio Match Company. Earlier, small match shops were known to have existed, of which one was started by John Wilson near River Styx. Wilson bought a simple match formula from a German and began manufacturing sticks dipped in a solution of sulfur, glue, water, ground shale, phosphorous and chlorate of potash. The formula was not too stable. As a result of its unpredictable nature, unwanted combustion was common. Wilson had difficulty in getting anyone to transport his matches because of the erratic combustion problem.

A second match manufacturing location was on North Lyman Street near Maple Street. Captain George Lyman saw the future in matches and tried to improve on previous formulae for making them. His stint was short-lived, a result of the Barber Match Company's starting in Barberton and a machine that E.J. Young had invented that would accelerate the process in making matches. Although he invented the new machine in 1893, Young waited until 1895 to build his first match shop in Wadsworth, fearing legal action if he were to infringe on patent rights that the Barber Match Company held (the rights would expire in 1895).

The first building that Young built was 50 by 180 feet, but he quickly had to build another one to increase the floor space more than threefold. Soon after, other buildings had to be added to support the meteoric rise in production and sales, the latter a story in itself.

As was stated in earlier accounts, the Pennsylvania Dutch were very clannish. E.J. Young and most of the other partners were of this ilk and used this trait to their advantage. Young was not the progenitor of this strategy, however. Milton Hershey, of Hershey chocolate fame, utilized the characteristic long before. Hershey reasoned that Pennsylvania Dutch workers would be pleased that their own people were becoming successful and, therefore, give loyalty to the leaders who were fostering this success. The leaders were paternalistic but firm, conditions that the Dutch understood and accepted. Labor problems were few. As a result, the company was able to prosper without the employees organizing. Young copied this strategy and enjoyed the worker loyalty it promised.

After the company grew almost exponentially, there was a need for other types of workers. People from Europe heard about the employment possibilities and came in relatively large numbers. The wages were low,

When the Match was in its infancy.

but the immigrants could function, even with language difficulties. Many of the immigrants moved into homes close to the shop, thereby saving transportation costs and obviating the necessity to invest in a car. Workers from all over Wadsworth generally walked to the Match. The shop was located at the bottom of Match Shop Hill. Going down was easy, but going back up at the end of a shift was more difficult. In the beginning, the sidewalks were made of wood and were slippery in the winter, making the trek even more difficult.

Needless to say, matches are incendiary products—a tiny explosive, as it were. Because of this, match manufacturers worked industriously to incorporate safety in matches. One of the reasons that the Ohio Match Company was so successful was that it retained the chemical expertise of Hugo Schapiro, a European-educated explosives expert, to develop a formula that would not include yellow phosphorus, since yellow phosphorus could cause fatalities in certain instances and was therefore illegal to use after 1913. Schapiro was able to achieve the measure of safety desired, making matches nonpoisonous.

Another feature to make matches safer was to place them into a closable cover—we now know them as book matches. The chemical composition, as well as the friction component of book matches, was such that the only way they would light would be to strike them on an emery attached to the flap. Stick matches could be ignited by striking them on any abrasive surface.

People who worked at the Match worked in "big stick," "wee-wees" or "book match." Although prominent throughout the factory in nearly every department, the book match operation used only women as a rule. Functioning as automatons in front of a line feeding them matches for eight hours a day, they would take thirteen books in one action and twelve in another, place them in a box and repeat the process time after time—all at lightning speed. Noise was overpowering in the department, since the "stitchers"—the machines that would stitch the matches to the cardboard cover—made a thunderous noise with every punch. This happened thousands of times each hour. Every few minutes, the line would shut down to give the women a short reprieve. Although stitchers were loud, they were not nearly as loud as the deafening silence that prevailed during the break.

The Match was ultimately purchased by Hunt Foods, Inc. in the 1950s, and at that time, manufacturing matches ceased in Wadsworth. It is now a "matchless city."

THE OHIO BOXBOARD COMPANY

The Ohio Boxboard Company, the fourth Ohio Company, came into existence when Ohio Match and Ohio Salt had difficulty getting enough cardboard for match- and saltboxes. In 1903, a few years after the Ohio Match and Salt Companies were founded, E.J. Young reasoned that if he manufactured his own cardboard, he could save money and sell his other products for less.

The Boxboard grew as rapidly as did the Match and Salt. Soon it was able to supply other vendors and became an entity unto itself, expanding upward for several years running.

Dr. Nathan S. Everhard was president of the Boxboard until his death in 1919, after which Edwin J. Young became president. Following his death in 1933, Wayne Young, E.J.'s son, took the reins until the company merged with Packaging Corporation of America in 1960.

Dr. Everhard and E.J. Young were cousins, as were Aaron Pardee and Burke Hinsdale, although the latter were first cousins and Everhard and Young were a bit more distant. This is significant in that Pardee and Hinsdale were descendants of the New England stock, while Everhard and Young were Pennsylvania Dutch. As was mentioned previously, the Pennsylvania Dutch were not exactly a welcomed people when they arrived shortly after the New Englanders came, but they prospered with their strong work ethic, frugality and strong urge for social cohesiveness. Perhaps it was this competition that caused both factions to prosper as they did.

Other industries in Wadsworth emerged but with less fanfare than was given the Ohio Companies. Smaller in scope but important in that their presence helped diversify the labor market in Wadsworth, these companies contributed greatly to the economic base of the village and, later, the city.

THE WADSWORTH BRICK AND TILE COMPANY

The Wadsworth Brick and Tile Company is located on a rich area of clay south of the village, about a quarter mile west of the north–south road, now officially called Main Street.

Bricks were first made in Wadsworth on the Hiram Yockey farm—presently a housing development—probably about 1850. The farm is a quarter square containing 160 acres, located on Silvercreek Road about a quarter mile north of Silvercrest Road. This operation lasted for several years but was abandoned

The early brickyard kilns.

when the Yockey family turned to farming entirely. In 1893, Yockey, or one of his offspring, built a barn that stood until the housing development emerged in the 1950s.

At least three other brickyards existed in the 1850s and a few years beyond: one at the end of Chestnut Street from 1874 to 1885; one at Clark Corners; and one in River Styx. Remnants of the latter are still visible. None of these is associated with Wadsworth Brick and Tile, founded in 1904.

William Ault, J.K. Durling, W.M. Wertz, Charles A. Curtis, E.S. Pardee and M.H. Leatherman—all local businessmen—were the stockholders. Almost unheard of for the time, the company produced about six million bricks annually. Shipping them was difficult since everything was done either by hand or with the use of horses. Notwithstanding local deliveries, bricks were shipped by rail, a somewhat easy process, since the railroad ran close to the property that the company owned.

The quality of clay was excellent. As a result, and with innovative minds during the tenure of Superintendent Wilbur Cook, the company added clay tile to the brick line. Clay tiles were covered with a vitreous substance for use in underground electric cables. Fort Knox, the depository of the nation's gold, buried all of its cable underground for safety purposes. Prior to the vitreous application, the tile would not survive beneath the ground. With the vitreous cover, however, it lasted significantly longer. Electricity for the nation's gold was protected by Wadsworth-made tiles.

The Excel Rubber Company

It is not surprising that Wadsworth would have some identification with rubber products since it is so close to the rubber capital of the world, Akron. In 1919, on a seventeen-acre tract southeast of the village and near the Erie Railroad tracks, the Excel Rubber Company, organized by Ross Trump, built a small plant that had a short life. In 1923, the plant was sold to the Studebaker-Wulff Rubber Company. The Grubb Rubber Company and Rex Rubber Company also had a short tenure of ownership. Finally, after going into receivership, the Wadsworth Merchants Association purchased the entire real estate for $25,000.

In 1928, the Wadsworth Mechants Association became stockholders in the Kemitex Products, Inc. venture. The company made window shades and came to Wadsworth after it had outgrown its capacity in Barberton, where it was associated with the Seiberling Rubber Company. After increasing its product line from window shades to other rubber products, it ceased to exist about 1940.

Close to the site of the now defunct Kemitex was the Bearfoot Sole Company, another rubber company that made soles for shoes and stocking protectors for Dr. Scholl's. The company was organized in Massachusetts and moved to Barberton, where it used space in the Seiberling Rubber Company. When space there was outgrown, it utilized the empty Kemitex building in addition to its space in Barberton. During World War II, Seiberling was

The Excel Rubber when it existed.

obliged to make more tires for the war effort and forced Bearfoot Rubber to move out.

The war effort affected production of the Bearfoot lines as well. The company was forced to make rain gear for the troops, food bags to protect edibles on the battlefield and other rubber products that would serve as protection for military purposes. After the war, it returned to making soles and heels, both crepe and molded rubber.

The Calvin family had a long association with the Bearfoot Sole Company.

Part IX

Personalities that Grew Wadsworth

Tommy Lucas, the One-Man Show

Tommy Lucas was, indeed, a native son. His father, Sam Lucas, owned the last farm on Silvercreek Road, bordered on the south by South Medina Line Road. Originally the farm expanded to the east as far as the East Medina Line Road; however, the *Historical Atlas of Medina County, 1874* shows a few lots on the latter road. This would imply that either Sam sold them off his farm or they had been allotted before he purchased the farm,

Tommy was born on the farm on May 23, 1883, the son of J.S. (Sam) and Susan Long Lucas, the daughter of a Wadsworth pioneer. Sam is credited for building houses and initiating a plan to accept monthly payments until the house was paid off—a form of "land contract" and a novel idea at the time.

Tommy is a legend in Wadsworth to this day. Those who are old enough remember his beginnings as a laborer in the coal mines, working at the Match, becoming the town marshal, being the first chief of police and, finally, becoming mayor. His political life was equally varied, having campaigned as a Socialist when he first ran for marshal, then as a Republican for the second term and as a Democrat when he ran for mayor.

He began his career as marshal by patrolling on a bicycle, earning only a dollar a day, or less if the month carried thirty-one days. Later, he rode a motorcycle, a gray one that had a small emergency light on it. It was not until he had been a law enforcement officer for twenty-six years that he drove the first police cruiser, a 1937 Ford, purchased by the city.

His formal education was meager, having attended the Number Eleven School on what is now Johnson Road for a short time and then the Weaverville School, located on the edge of his family's farm. He finally completed eight years of education. Nonetheless, his keen and perceptive mind had no equal in ferreting out malefactors, and he was heralded as one of the top law enforcement officers in the area.

Mothers used him as a threat, as did teachers and townspeople. It was not uncommon for parents to tell their children that if they didn't behave, they would call Tommy Lucas. Teachers were heard to do the same thing in schools, and local businesses would ward off would-be thieves by voicing a quick mention of his name.

During the first couple decades of his career, he patrolled the village alone. Then, in 1938, he had four helpers—three full-time officers and one substitute patrolman. His "jail" was in the basement of Smith's Cleaners on the square, just north of the East Park and about two hundred feet from High Street. It was not until 1936 that he had some decent quarters and a holding cell in the basement of the new city hall.

As if he did not have enough to occupy his time—on call twenty-four hours a day, seven days a week—he was also the sanitation officer. During the 1918 flu epidemic, he was also the quarantine officer. Added to an almost impossible schedule, he was the truant officer, albeit without too much activity, since the students feared his capture.

Lucas Court is named in his honor. It is where he lived and built homes for his children. While living there during Prohibition days, the story is told about his having gone to the outside privy one night, not suspecting any danger. It was not until later that he learned that two of his arrestees were lying in wait for him. Fortunately, they did not execute their intentions, but suffice it to say, he had many in the village who were not pleased with his swift, yet fair, correction measures.

He knew every miscreant in the village. A story is told by one perpetrator, who, as of this writing, is in his upper eighties: The Wadsworth Library had Indian artifacts in a room behind where books were shelved. On a halcyon summer day, the teenager and some other friends went into the museum section where the artifacts were located, pretending to be interested in the arrowheads, bows, skulls, scalps, etc. In truth, they were there to unlock a window so they could sneak back in at night to take one of the skulls for some fun. That night, they did indeed take one of the skulls and planted it in the flower bed of a spinster who was an avid gardener. The following day, when the lady started digging in her flower bed, she felt something hard beneath the ground and thought it was a rock. Upon further investigation, she was mortified to discover that it was a skull. She ran to the police station that was just down the street and reported it to Tommy Lucas. Unflustered, Tommy went directly to the store where the perpetrator's father was and

Tommy Lucas, a legend in his own time.

asked where his son was. Upon learning of his whereabouts, Tommy went to the house and got an immediate confession from the boy.

Tommy had a reputation for solving crimes through intuition. Perhaps the many years of being the only law enforcer taught him what present-day police learn academically.

Nellie Harter

Nellie Augusta Harter was the first and only woman to become an editor of a Wadsworth newspaper. Additionally, she was probably the first woman to serve as a bank director. Above these achievements, however, is her national standing as having been the person who secured free postage for the millions of servicemen and servicewomen during World War II.

She was born on April 13, 1886, in adjoining Guilford Township, the daughter of William and Eliza Peters Harter and the granddaughter of Christian and Mary Long Peters, early settlers in Wadsworth.

After her graduation from Wadsworth High School, she taught school but had her mind set on becoming a journalist. In 1904, she began to realize her dream by becoming a hand typesetter for the *Wadsworth Banner* but quickly moved up to writing stories. She had a fond admiration for the house of the *Banner*'s publisher, William Swisher. Her fascination turned into reality a quarter of a century later when she purchased the house and lived in it until it was razed to build the fire station in 1962.

In 1906, when Edwin Day purchased the *Press* and *Banner* and combined them into the *Banner-Press*, she went to work for the *Barberton Telegram* for one year but returned to Wadsworth the following year when the paper changed hands again, with Walter Hostetler now the owner.

Journalistic staff was meager in those days, to say the least. At one point, when Nellie was only twenty-four years old, she found herself alone with an edition to print and did so without help. She wanted to become a journalist with a big city paper, but Hostetler convinced her to stay. She did and bought a one-quarter interest in the paper from the meager salary she had earned from working there. She bought another one-quarter interest later and, upon Mr. Hostetler's death, purchased the entire paper in 1935.

In an editorial during World War II, Nellie urged that service personnel be permitted to send letters postage-free while in uniform. The editorial was enriched with countless letters of support, all urging the same sentiment. Before long, Washington was overrun with letters, and President Roosevelt approved the measure. As a result, it is estimated that several million letters sent by service people reached their destinations with the word *FREE* where the stamp normally would go.

Nellie's efforts did not go unnoticed by the federal government. In 1943, the *Banner-Press* was honored with the Herrick Award for being the weekly newspaper with more than two thousand subscribers that made the "most outstanding" contribution to the morale of the nation.

Mention was made of Nellie as being the first and only woman of that time to serve on the board of a bank. She received another national prize in 1934 for her efforts in reopening the Wadsworth Savings and Trust Company in 1933 as the Citizens Bank of Wadsworth. She added these two honors to sixteen state prizes that she received for newspaper production.

Nellie Harter, Wadsworth's grand lady.

After forty years of a career in journalism and after having won so many awards for her excellence in writing, Nellie sold the paper to H.J. Hall in 1944. In her final editorial, she said that the paper had been the bread, meat and recreation of her life.

So it was, also, for Wadsworth.

ELLA EVERHARD

Wadsworth has had a long line of "libraries," dating back to the days of the first settlers; however, none found a permanent residence or had an appropriate setting.

In 1922, the Wadsworth Federation of Women's Clubs offered fifty dollars to explore the possibility of a permanent library for the community. With the miniscule amount it collected in addition to the fifty dollars it had, the club did not have enough to purchase books. The Education Committee of the club decided to borrow two hundred books from the state library and place them in the then high school (now the intermediate school), where the principal and superintendent had their offices. Although this was intended to be a "public" library, the books were used essentially by the high school students.

Noting that the arrangement at the high school was not workable for the public, the club moved the books to a small room in the building located on the northeast corner of the square, known as the Albrecht Building. The "librarians" were volunteers from the women's club. When the room became overcrowded again, the books were moved to a larger room reserved for Mayor Fred Falk's office. Mayor Falk reasoned that his office would be better served as a library since he was a part-time mayor and was not there much of the time.

In 1924, girl scouts went from door to door in the village and collected about seven hundred books and about thirty dollars for the library. With many of these books being at a low reading difficulty level, they were best suited for children. Miss Carolyn Treffinger, principal of Franklin School and a children's book author herself, conducted story hours for children, thereby building the love for reading in children, a love that was sometimes transferred to older members of their families.

It was at this point that Ella Finley Everhard purchased the Dr. Thomas C. Leiter House on the north side of Broad Street, about two hundred feet west of Lyman Street, and donated it to the village for a permanent library. As a condition of the gift, Mrs. Everhard asked that the house also serve as a meeting place for women's cultural activities. Although there was no money to fund the library, the $17,000 gift of the house was a good start.

It would be appropriate to tell about the life of the donor, Ella Everhard. She was born across the road from the Wadsworth Township line in Chippewa Township to highly educated parents. Her father, William Finley, was a professor and head of Romance languages (French, Spanish and Italian) at Washington and Jefferson College. Her mother, Rhonda Harris, was a descendant of the first settler in Stark County.

Ella attended a one-room school with a few other students, one of whom was Nathan Everhard. After her local education days, she went to Mendota, Illinois, to a Lutheran college to become a teacher. She taught in Bethel, Missouri, for a year and then returned to the area to marry her one-room-school classmate, Nathan. They moved to 180 Main Street in Wadsworth, where her now physician husband began his practice of medicine. They never left Wadsworth and contributed greatly to its success. In addition to donating the building for the library, they donated heavily to the new Grace Lutheran Church when it was built in the teens. The Everhard Lodge at the YMCA Camp Craig is named in their honor. When the Salvation Army needed a building, Dr. Everhard led the challenge with money and talent and provided it with a building in the south end.

In the Leiter House, the first floor was dedicated to the library with a room in the back for American Indian artifacts. The second floor had a small auditorium that accommodated modest groups of people, particularly ladies' clubs. Ella was a member of the Federation of Women's Clubs, the overarching group that included the Followers of Pallas Athene, the Art and History club, the Sorosis club and the Literature and Arts club. The carriage house behind the main house was given to the Girl Scouts for its activities.

It was appropriate for the federation to be housed in the library. During the Great Depression of the 1930s, the women collected books, gave monetary donations to the library and served as volunteers, since the village could not support these activities financially.

The site of the Leiter House is the exact spot where Judge Frederick Brown deposited his personal library in 1816, two years after the first settlers arrived. The forefathers had the vision; those who followed fulfilled the vision; and those now living magnify the vision.

Bibliography

Erie Railroad magazine. "The Erie." August 1948.

Hinsdale, Mary L., ed. *Garfield-Hinsdale Letters*. Ann Arbor: University of Michigan Press, 1949.

Historical and Business Directory of Wadsworth, Ohio. Wadsworth, OH: Enterprise Print, 1870.

Historical Atlas of Medina County Ohio, 1874. Medina, OH: L.H. Everets and Company, 1874.

Historical Sketch of Sacred Heart Church, Wadsworth. Diocese of Cleveland. Wadsworth, OH: Banner-Press, 1936.

Lile, Nancy. "Early Driving Days Recalled by Pioneer Akron Auto Owner." *Akron (OH) Beacon Journal*, July 29, 1948.

Medina County Historical Society. *The History of Medina County*. Fostoria, OH: Gray Printing Co., 1948.

Rohrer, Anna Lois. *Mennonites of Medina County: 150 Years, 1832–1982*. Wadsworth, OH: Bethel Mennonite Church, 1982.

Schapiro, Eleanor I., ed. *Wadsworth Center to City*. Wadsworth, OH: Banner-Press, 1938.

———, ed. *Wadsworth Heritage.* Wadsworth, OH: Wadsworth News-Banner, 1964.

Stafford, Bob. "Andy Auble, First U.S. Garageman." *Akron (OH) Beacon Journal*, April 23, 1932.

Wadsworth Village Council. "General Ordinances of the City of Wadsworth." Wadsworth, OH: Steam Printing House, 1876.

About the Author

Born in Wadsworth, Ohio, on January 5, 1931, Dr. Caesar Carrino (pictured here with his wife, Lynda) attended Wadsworth schools, graduating in 1948. He earned a bachelor's degree before serving in the military and master's and doctorate degrees later.

Beginning in 1954, he taught in the Norton Schools, became principal in 1956, functioned as a supervisor in Summit County schools in 1966 and joined the University of Akron in 1967. In 1970, he became assistant to the dean of the College of Education, assistant dean in 1972 and was then promoted to dean of the Evening College and Summer Sessions in 1974. He retired in 1989.

Following retirement, he trained industrialists, served as principal of two schools, became a high school chancellor, advised at-risk students, directed a Professional Education unit and became mayor of Wadsworth in 2000.

Presently, he works with Historic Downtown Wadsworth to help preserve its historic integrity and audits American university programs for accreditation.